I0013930

Backpacking with GPS in Mauritius

Nabee Yasir

Backpacking with GPS in Mauritius

Engineering project in technology- GPS & web programming

VDM Verlag Dr. Müller

Impressum/Imprint (nur für Deutschland/ only for Germany)

Bibliografische Information der Deutschen Nationalbibliothek: Die Deutsche Nationalbibliothek verzeichnet diese Publikation in der Deutschen Nationalbibliografie; detaillierte bibliografische Daten sind im Internet über http://dnb.d-nb.de abrufbar.

Alle in diesem Buch genannten Marken und Produktnamen unterliegen warenzeichen-, marken- oder patentrechtlichem Schutz bzw. sind Warenzeichen oder eingetragene Warenzeichen der jeweiligen Inhaber. Die Wiedergabe von Marken, Produktnamen, Gebrauchsnamen, Handelsnamen, Warenbezeichnungen u.s.w. in diesem Werk berechtigt auch ohne besondere Kennzeichnung nicht zu der Annahme, dass solche Namen im Sinne der Warenzeichen- und Markenschutzgesetzgebung als frei zu betrachten wären und daher von jedermann benutzt werden dürften.

Coverbild: www.purestockx.com

Verlag: VDM Verlag Dr. Müller Aktiengesellschaft & Co. KG
Dudweiler Landstr. 99, 66123 Saarbrücken, Deutschland
Telefon +49 681 9100-698, Telefax +49 681 9100-988, Email: info@vdm-verlag.de
Zugl.: University of Portsmouth, Project for BSc(Hons) Technology Management and Computing, 2009.

Herstellung in Deutschland:
Schaltungsdienst Lange o.H.G., Berlin
Books on Demand GmbH, Norderstedt
Reha GmbH, Saarbrücken
Amazon Distribution GmbH, Leipzig
ISBN: 978-3-639-19870-6

Imprint (only for USA, GB)

Bibliographic information published by the Deutsche Nationalbibliothek: The Deutsche Nationalbibliothek lists this publication in the Deutsche Nationalbibliografie; detailed bibliographic data are available in the Internet at http://dnb.d-nb.de .

Any brand names and product names mentioned in this book are subject to trademark, brand or patent protection and are trademarks or registered trademarks of their respective holders. The use of brand names, product names, common names, trade names, product descriptions etc. even without a particular marking in this works is in no way to be construed to mean that such names may be regarded as unrestricted in respect of trademark and brand protection legislation and could thus be used by anyone.

Cover image: www.purestockx.com

Publisher:
VDM Verlag Dr. Müller Aktiengesellschaft & Co. KG
Dudweiler Landstr. 99, 66123 Saarbrücken, Germany
Phone +49 681 9100-698, Fax +49 681 9100-988, Email: info@vdm-publishing.com

Printed in the U.S.A.
Printed in the U.K. by (see last page)
ISBN: 978-3-639-19870-6

EXECUTIVE SUMMARY

Backpaking with gps, was a great project to work with. I had the opportunities to know about the countryside, how the geo positioning systems work, and how it can prove to be useful to people. Many approaches can now be used, to contribute to the society, either in Mauritius, or abroad. The abilities of precise positioning, referencing, makes routes, pathways directly accessible to, and with google's new approach to public development, the interactions of gps, google earth and maps are becoming widely popular.

The project developed mainly consumed software resources from the internet, with virtual schooling in programming, and free, and public codes for developers. The approach was modern, through producing a pilot website, whereby functionalities such as relating a database of coordinates to maps, was made through modular designing and development. The outcome was good, as website pilot project, can show updated points of restaurants, sightseeing, with many other exotic places as well as strategic ones. Anyone can upload points from a gps, and plot routes to find their way. Due to time constraints, and juggling efforts between professional work, overall implementation came successful, though with minor miscellaneous errors. The final project, integrated, fits in different systems in future endeavors, such as a social community of school children, blind people with voiced handheld gps, or automated vehicle guidance. Research, foreseeing and attempting in engineering, opens avid ways for progress to our civilizations and we contribute, by learning, participaticing, vividly.

ACKNOWLEDGEMENTS

I owe completing this project to many dear ones as much as individuals, as institutes. First and foremost, to purpletrain.com, the prompt requests replies, and all my different module lecturers, that took the time to understand, bear with us, the persistent questions. Purpletrain, is an excellent experience, for us, who mix professional work with studies. Topped with uk's greatest university, Portsmouth,will always be a leading name & a learning standard for us to remember, throughout our lifetime. Hard work, mixing daily life, professional achievements, with academic studies, reveals to us, the being of responsible citizens of tomorrow, in a global world of technology. I really appreciate it today, as completing a bachelors degree, makes us only stronger, sculpting our skills as well as our personality.

My first heartedly thanks to our project lecturer, who made this completion successful. My second thoughts are towards my family, my brother, mum, and late father who strieved hard to make me stand where I am today. I also owe a lot of encouragements from my friends, in life, who have been really encouraging me to go for a bachelors degree. Last, but not least, the university of Portsmouth online friends, and PT friends all around the world.

May god be with us, all the way,

Nabee Yasir,

Mauritius, Indian Ocean.   Email: cheers@intnet.mu

TABLE OF CONTENTS

CHAPTER 1

INSIGHT

The tourism industry has been simmering with innovations & quality services since the last decades. Since, the global recession gulped part of the industry's clients, and hence, one of the challenges was, to re-engineer a project that could help promote the industry further to, with the lowest possible resources, while being close to reality. Mauritius is a fascinating country, often spoken as a paradise, and seen as a fairytale, with whitish beaches warm lagoon waters, all within the safe, richness of our coral reefs. We have excellent communication channels, cellular phone links to all parts of the island, high speed internet bandwidth, excellent lodging service, road networks, and a free democratic political stability. As a tropical island, we foster indigenous plants and exotic green environment and that dazzles Europeans and people living far from the tropics. Though these are unseen rare environments, coupled with developed citizenship and technology, we had habits only to expose information to the high class clients, and this project will approach the accessibility of information, to a grand public, outside the country, wishing to enliven their stays.

INTRODUCTION

Backpakers and GPS in Mauritius, is aimed to address the needs of backpakers, coming into our paradise island. Having once built a solid reputation of first-class tourism, Mauritius is now in a conjunction of global recession, and feels attracting middle-class tourists, as support to the tourism industry. Often people do not know where they are coming, until they land into the national airport, or on the hotel doormat. Once arrived, they are held by hotel accommodations and tour operators, who usually, take them out, without any particular taste of what tour, or how the journeys would be like. Backpackers and middle class tourists, plan their own holidays, and as there is no availability of information, for free trips planning, this project will address such needs, being a complementary resource for backpakers and middle class tourism.

SITUATION OVERVIEW

Mauritius has the excellent environment to promote tourism industry. Being a tropical island, with varying temperatures of around 20-35 degrees, we foster white sandy beaches, calm blue lagoons, as well as green places. Crocodile rearing, walking with lions, biking, quad biking, sea parachutes, water skiing, beach volleys, swims, undersea walks, diving are amongst the activities, one can practise.

These activities vary from place to place, and incomers realise the availability of such services depending on which regions or whoever tour operator they are assigned to, only when they arrive in Mauritius. Most tourists, embark into a chartered vacation plan, having little choice of their own visits, depending entirely on their initial booking, or on other people's choice.

Websites, on internet is one of the major means to communicate with the world. As a communication tool, many have created websites, but most, represent scattered information, with little or no contacts or route guides around the island. If, someone, could have a charter, before coming to Mauritius, if he can plan his own visits, his own tours, rent cars, or schedules, it can provide him with flexibility and choice and a feeling of being at home, all within the island's cultural habits.

THE PROBLEM

Mauritius is a tropical island, with lots of activities, and leisure. Even though, tourism is open market, incomers find themselves often jammed, in a tour already programmed. They often do not know the places around Mauritius, and cannot really choose what is worth of their sacred annual holiday visits. In fact, most of the time, it is travel agencies and tour operators plan that their holidays. Some while returning, may have seen a part of the island, and yet, another one, may have discovered another façade.

It is felt that, tourists would feel much better, if they could plan their own holidays, in Mauritius. Booking of hotels, would remain traditional means, and on the other hand, they can spend their journeys on their own, either in taxis, contract cars, or even tours.

Through such services and infrastructure that is already in place, information must be readily available, and accessible. Information must be first collected, and gathered in a suitable manner, so as tourists, incomers or backpakers find the ease to orient themselves across the island. The means to representing information, will be the best outfit, into web form. Information ingredients, such as route plans, sight seeing places, beaches, lodgings, fuelling would be a a good mix, of producing a website. Some web places that exist already, show part of these info, or very little. An example is www.grandbaie.mu, that represents a single village in Mauritius, although it only shows a part of the island's culture.

Being able to represent the entire island, with different perspectives, blends, flavors and spots, may change the way people think about Mauritius, and naturally may contribute in making their holidays and trip plans only better. Ideally, the points of interests would be accessible places, with details, may be part of the contribution, in making holidays more interesting. What to see, and where, are the common questions of any holiday planner. Further to, it can, as well promote leisure activities, at a national perspective.

SCOPE OF WORK

Collecting data, handling and processing the information, is an essential kick off point. Textual information as restaurant mini records, locations (coordinates & geometry), photographs and maps would be amongst the usual processes. The idea, is to build a site, that loads maps, information, places of interests as updated and lively as can be, in view to support holiday planning with GPS in Mauritius. Here, a planned stepped report of the methodologies used, actions and development will ensure the scope of work is met.

STRATEGIC VALUE

Building up a communication place for tourists, is an interesting perspective for holiday planners. Business-wise, it can help to promote middle class tourists in Mauritius, as well as consolidate the average income earnt from tourist industry, during the global recession. It can, along the way, flourish, the income earned of medium and small businesses, that spinning around our big tourism industry. The strategic value, of the project, lies on the basis of foreigners, mixing in the lives of Mauritians, through aequate information offered. The project may also foster the internal tourism trades, such as bungalow owners, inland restaurants and other service oriented spices of the island.

AIMS & OBJECTIVES

Aims

Aim is to make use of suitable technologies, to create a website that may contribute to the average incoming middle class tourists in Mauritius. This so, in view to promote our island, through means to communicate information such as places of interest, contacts, pictures and mapping layers of the country's routes. The web layout will be an instructive material, to backpackers and travelers and even inland sight seers.

Objectives in meeting the aim

The objectives to be met are: First is to find suitable maps, and digitizing them in a suitable format, and hence, layering proceeds. To feed the maps with information, data collection needs to be done and Google Earth, will be an aid to such development, and well as a GPS device, to record precise geometric places. Another step involves collecting the data, compacting and storage, for further use. Pictures, textual information and coordinates throughout the island will be collected and hence, given a treat, to fit in, a web display. Contact with service suppliers, inland tourism companies, and private bungalow are some of the contacts to be established. In the final touch, assembling all the information, a mini database of records, maps and coordinates, will be the ultimate tasks to render an accessible and easy to use website.

Chapters overview

Chapter Two: Introduction of middle class tourism in Mauritius, gathering information, competitors, products, tools and summary

Chapter Three: defining requirements & services, needs, tools. Hence, proceeding to selection of required, evaluation, drafting on the full requirements specification, and summary

Chapter Four(design): The design objectives to be met.

Chapter Five(implementation): creation & assembly of the website, with information store. Refine and revise the working model.

Chapter Six(testing): Provides the test plan, test cases and results.

Chapter Seven(Evaluations)- a critical approach, to evaluating what was created, constructed and its impact, and what has been learnt.

Chapter Eight(Conclusion): Summing up the project & future perspectives.

Miscellaneous(Appendices & referencing): All documents annexed, for the project & websites, documents read and misc articles inspired to write up project.

SUMMARY

The first chapter, is an overview of the project's different phases, what focus will be onto, the selection of such, and how it will be tackled. Chapters have been defined, will be further written, to meet the objectives, adhering to the scope proposed. Lastly, chapter one, is an overview of how the report, will be written, as closing up with the different sets of objectives, through each chapter, that is yet to be drafted.

CHAPTER 2

LITERATURE REVIEW

BRIEF

Tourists have been arriving at an increasing rate in Mauritius, since the early 80's. We now accommodate around one million incomers per year, and we are planning to develop the industry into a 4 million incomer business, on a yearly scale.

As stated(World Travel and Tourism Council, 2009), the " *contribution of Travel & Tourism to Gross Domestic Product is expected to rise from 25.4% (MUR77.3 bn or US$2,542.3 mn) in 2009 to 27.5% (MUR202.7 bn or US$5,379.2 mn) by 2019* ". From these, generating employments, contributions to growth and exports, follows an increasing rate, and we can say that the peak to attaining a 4 million incomer industry, is merely on its may.

Link:
http://www.wttc.org/eng/Tourism_Research/Tourism_Economic_Research/Country _Reports/Mauritius/

Here, the rising rate, may indeed require more services and information for better support of incoming tourists. Lets have a glance, of the aspects and services that the tourism industry offers:

- Ecotourism: nature parks, wildlife sight seeing, quad biking, golf courses, gardens.
- Beach & Water sports: Skiing, Fishing, Parasailing, Diving, swimming, Surfing, sun bathing, beach volley.
- Lodging: Luxury/small/medium hotels, Inland lodges, bungalows, beach apartments.
- Restaurants & food: markets, classy & medium restaurants, food outlets.
- Mobility & communication: Cellular phones(easy prepaid buying), and contract vehicles are available at different points of the island.

The defined information about the country needs to be gathered, and presented into web form, so as to appeal tourists, to use and exploit the activities of the island, through a modern façade, using GPS and a resources database, in view to meet the aims and objectives. The following pages will provide a structured way, to gather the information discussed previously.

GATHERING DATA

Gathering information have particulars at each major tasks, needing a detailed sub-task plan. Fitting all into web displays, in a suitable form, fulfilling the needs, must be also defined. Methods, tools, materials used, will be elaborated here, so as to have a clear picture of what resources and limitations are presently available.

DATA

Different phases of data collection is imperative, to gather up all the corresponding and form up information. Classifying the different fields, we have:

- Collecting data from owners, sites, requests within the island.
- Collecting land marks (gps plots)
- Photos and other captures

Methods will be used to categorise each level of information requested, through:

- ❖ Interviews, transcript on paper records(places around the island)
- ❖ GPS marks and transcripts
- ❖ Picture storage

METHODS

Further defining the methods proposed, and the importance of it, below:

Interviews, transcript on paper records:

Interviews are important, as they reveal opinions of people, and interactions, either by phone, or in contact. Interviewing, also can open up areas of discussion, that makes a clearer picture of the topic.

In this part, phone interviews will replace the traditional methods of getting at the interviewees place. Instead, calling them will be a more convenient method. It will save time, and hence, allow more indepth questioning of the system. The only inconvenience would be, facial expressions, emotions cannot be witnessed over the phone. Still, onsite interviews will also be scheduled, in important meetings and discussions. Complementary actions will be transcripting into notes, the data collected. The step, adheres to collecting information about the countryside, of places of sightseeing around the island.

GPS marks and transcripts

GPS marks are the key data points. Each location, can be identified through a GPS landmark, that is latitude and longitude. Futher, to, with a located point, we can exactly "pin" it, on a map, and show it on web. For instance, a fuelling point, may have a unique latitude and longitunal record. Name, address, location, and telephone numbers, will be also part of a record, as secondary data.

GPS landmarks must be captured, collected, on transcript that is paper records. Further to, learn about route paths, and other corresponding information blending. Hospitals locations, clinics can be part of a collection of records, as an example. Another one, would be the location of restaurants around the island. All, within a stated set of fields, the records collection is annexed in the appendix section, which will later be transformed into map coordinates.

Picture Storage

Pictures of the island, will also be taken, in view to show the beautiful countryside, and coastal regions. Pictures needs consequent amount of storage and also rendering. Applications, such as photoshop, will be used, further on, to provide better quality of images, and suitable formats for website making. Along, with a picture, is it sought to capture the address, with a small description, counting as a record, shown along in the appendix section.

The methods describe, shall be acted upon, to capture what is needed and further to, act as a baseline of suitable information, for a proper design and development stage.

TOOLS   & SELECTION RATIONALS

Hardware

Aligned with methods of data collections, some materials are to be necessary and important for the process:

- ✓ digital camera, about 2.0 megapixel
- ✓ Mini GPS tracker-Garmin nuvi 205
- ✓ Notebook/paper records type

Digital camera, will be for taking series of pictures, complementing the picture storage methodology. The Garmin nuvi 205, which is a handheld, precise device to locate GPS landmarks, will be used to capture coordinates of each records, and transcripted on paper, for later use. It can also be saved, downloaded, and treated digital-wise.

Software

Software, is the "pillar" part in web construction. Once the data collection process done, software needs, will have to be met, in view to achieving implementation. Let us draw a concern line, a broad view, of what we expect to have, as software needs, at this first stage:

- ✓ Photo rendering software-adobe
- ✓ Website making software-html, asp, php
- ✓ Map manipulations-Google earth/maps, and miscellaneous free wares
- ✓ -GPS imports/exports applications
- ✓ -Database engine-sql/access

Notes

Hardware, drives the software applications, and is as cohesive in the process, as glue. Though hardware and software needs will be described in detail in chapter three, it is wise to have a snapshot, of the resources we need to prepare to go ahead:

- ➢ Internal/ External storage
- ➢ Processing- Ideally a Pentium core2duo with 2 Gb of Ram, 128Mb graphics cards,Usb slots, and dvd drive
- ➢ Security-physical lockup/authentications

Networking

Internet : connection to world wide web, ADSL 512 preferably.

Most essential, for documenting, finding resources, and website making, it will be of usage, as from the design chapters, and having a permanent, dedicated connection is the ideal tool.

Costing

Funding of the project, is the main spinal chord of turning into reality, any project. Funds being of second importance to achieving the aims, is yet a critical factor to achieving success. The more we have funds, better the project may be, in certain cases, but for this one, we will focus on simple tools that have been proposed earlier, along with a markup, to catch up with any uncertain expense. The funding will be done, mostly by myself, as I did not contact any sponsors at this time. A brief of what we expect to spend, as follows:

Software:

Operating system(windows XP)	already available
Database(sql or access)	already available
Photo(adobe)	Upon need
Website making(php,java,asp..)	free resources
Miscellaneous(licenses for utils etc)	Rs 5,000

Total cost: Rs   5,000

Hardware

Pentium IV	already available
Backup store(ext)	Rs 2,000
Security(physical) lock/password	Room
Digital camera	Available
GPS device	Rs 10,000
ADSL connection(I year)	Rs 8,000
Miscellaneous	Rs 5,000

Total: Rs   25,000

Grand total(hardware+software)   Rs   30,000

THE WEB COMPETITION

The World Wide Web, a free resource connecting the world, is a major marketplace for all tourism stakeholders. The fact that it is free makes it an available platform for people to communicate & acquaint. More, it represents a mere view of places around the world. These aspects, some have overexploited, ruining pictures (modifying) and writing any kind of articles, since there exists no copyright authorities for web posting. Hence, it makes the free virtual marketplace, a spot of uncertainty, in communication.

Web postings, are millions in figures. Many earn their living from it: making websites, advertising, writing articles, propaganda, are amongst others the means of disseminating information to the virtual world. Through these, tourism articles are one of the major fields of interest. Another instance is that, many operators, individuals use the internet as a resource to promote their properties and services. Mauritians also follow these trends, and often it is a profitable source of advertising, to attract tourists. Operators, service providers, hotel groups are all on the web, with the contact, and even booking information. Foreigners can contact them, with emails, fax, and telephone calls or perform online booking. But each entity mentioned, has its own web space, with the services he offers. Very few websites offer services that comprises of the entire parts of the country, or most services that one can get in Mauritius. Out of these few, we have selected a group of websites, for indepth analysis, as to what the competitors are offering:

- www.tourism-mauritius.mu
- http://www.grandbaie.mu
- www.mauritius.net
- http://www.islandinfo.mu

Competitors have many aims, and have been present since the opening of the World Wide Web to public. They each have their intents on promoting parts of the island, either from a lucrative point of view, or based upon reputation. Here, a blend of websites, have been collected, in view to analyse what content they offer and how they present information. Though this, we can find their aims, and rather, compare with what the project is proposing. The detailed analysis pages, are into the appendix, and a brief encounter, follows.

Analysis

Collecting data, and information about the competitors, has been the first task, in order to have a broader view of what they are doing, and how they have set themselves to. Budget allocations, funds, and motives that have been the prior aims, will be discussed through this part. Several points, will be also included, so as to assess them, and find out which market segments they are aiming. Annexed in the Appendix, is a short brief of the competitors' characteristics.

First and foremost, let us consider the motives. Most websites have their motives, aims and incentives derived. most of the tourist attraction websites, exists mainly for lucrative reasons. Either a company wants to promote Mauritius, as a destination, swallowing them to its services, or directing them to specific areas of interests. Such is done, as a means to earn money, or increase profitability within their enterprise. www.islandinfo.mu and www.mauritius .net are clear examples of promoting tourism, towards an enterprise, or a profitable goal. The more users contact & book places, the better the business runs; a clean set of B2C(business to client) objective.   Other motives also prevail, like promoting cultures, environments of the island, in view to desirable popularity. Growing the island's popularity, makes a solid reputation. As we need a good reputation to globally compete, with competitors like Seychelles islands, nation organisations have taken up the responsibilities of promoting Mauritius, as a world class destination. Such, not only promotes culture, but also, enhances regional trade. Intents like these, are natured by the www.tourism-mauritius.mu. Commonly known in Mauritius as the Mauritius tourism promotion agency, it has as aim to uplift Mauritius, amongst the best tourism destinations. As fallback for such intents, Mauritius earns, as more tourists come, and it helps our economy to blossom. An aspect of B2B, calling other businesses to accommodate in our graceful environment, as well as B2C. Instances of growing popularity, are also, promoting villages, that accomodates tourists. The more tourists are accommodated within a village, the more prosperous it becomes. Here, www.grandbaie.mu is one of the most populated tourist village in Mauritius. the intention, still a particular form of business to client(B2C)

The nuts and bolts, of websites mentioned. Most of the competitors have brilliant designs. Flash, java scripts, made much elegance, and clickable features. Adverts within, have made them even more colourful and attractive. It is definitely a fact that competitors have outsourced their websites, to developers, or website builders around the corners of the island. Although the splendid attractive layouts, the websites do not provide much detailed information about stay places, or even for back packers in Mauritius. More, addresses of where to go, in case of emergencies are not available. This ponders well a situation of what a tourist does, in case of emergencies, or in times of trouble. Here again, we denote the maximum of commercial information, with little provision of contacts, or taxi services around the island.

On overall, most sites represent what commercially is available in Mauritius, with few touching the sense of culture, or practicability, or even accessibility. The web advertising, makes someone go directly into a hotel room, as he doesn't know how to travel, or the whereabouts of the island: a user segment, of which my project is targeting. As the analysis of the competitors denotes here, the market has not been exploited yet, and mauritians as well as foreigners, may well appreciate the fact of having a non-for-profit, website with specific locations, and how to travel.

Application build

While analyzing the competitors, we can further understand that the aims and objectives are within scope, having a market of interested users on web. Also, we can elaborate from, that the is indeed project is realizable. With the least possible costs incurred, and free language development tools, a simple set of methods, can lead to a clean pilot system, of what is expected. Based upon these, an insight of the application build can be derived, and further dealt with, in the chapter four. The main steps in building and designing the web would be:

- Html pages, as graphical user interface
- ASP providing links to database
- Gallery of images
- Database records
- Maps and information

HTML pages: html is a simple language, helping to present and format web displays. Further to it is easy to link and hyperlink parts, or other sites within. The reason of choosing html, as a graphical interface, is that it is fairly simple to development, and most widely used. As, it is popular, documentation & instructions can easily be found on the web, it is an ideal tool to build a graphical user interface.

ASP: is a free open source language scripting language. It combines with HTML, and the language is comparable to C or java. Through previous experience in diploma level, I have tackled java, and C, thus making it an acquirable step to enhance developing capabilities. ASP will be mainly used to linking databases, storage and retrieval purposes, helping to deliver graphical user interface.

Gallery of images: a store of images has been mentioned. The store will initially trigger images flow, and uploading on website. Further to, it is aligned with the hardware needs, as image stores needs consequent amount of spacing.

Maps and layers: Maps will be layered with simple information, That is records collected and presented in a suitable form.

The entire combined, will make up a nice blend, to realizing the project. Throughout chapters 3 and 4, further defining the applications build, will be dealt with, going through the details, and further enhancing the plan of the final product.

Overview of Tools

The products to be used in building the system are quite simple materials. First, a recording device will be needed, such as a GPS, which records likely tourists spots and places of re-fuelling. Second instance, a digital camera, with an adequate storage space, would be most appropriate. At last, but not least, are the computing requirements. A strong pc, with capability if handling photos and maps, will be a needy resource for the upholding of the model website.

Software requirements are also important. They will render pictures, and refine the project accordingly. A windows license is the first requirement. After, we will need photoshop, google earth, and other GPS software converters(importing and exporting such). An Adsl line, would be also in the requirements, 512 kpbs, permanent internet line that delivers internet connection all round the clock.

SUMMARY

This chapter provides an overview of the similar projects, that have already been developed, and what the contents represents. Contents, which when analysed, have been either on a lucrative aim, leisure portals and lifestyles. In most cases, these projects provide very few information to the general public, or they focus information, as per their business reaches. In comparison to the project development proposed, the information is intended in an opened way, to the general public, regardless of the class of tourism coming to Mauritius.

The tools to be used have been described, and further to their availabilities. Most of the tools, I already have, which represents the minimum investment requirements, some software available on web, like google earth(registration member needy), and photo rendering software is readily available on my pc.

To sum up, the information provided by chapter two, makes it easier to tackle the project, since no major competitors are available, that is, competitors with the same aims. The availability of resources are more than adequate, and inland activities are on the grip(information ready to be gathered):

Tools & materials needed			
Type	Category	Description	Availability
PC	Hardware	P 4, with storage	available
Digital Camera	Hardware	2.0 megapixel, 2gb store	ready to use
GPS	Hardware	Handheld, garmin nuvi models	to buy
Operating system	Software	Windows XP	available
Editors	Software	Office 2007 standard	ready to use
Photo editors	Software	Adobe	to install
Maps	Software	Google earth, Gmaps	ready to use
Mapping software	Software	free web utilities	to download
Storage	Software	Access 2007	ready to use
Internet	Network	ADSL 512 k	ready to use

CHAPTER 3

REQUIREMENTS

INTRODUCTION

The steps in this chapter, are to defining the requirements of the project. The requirements, comprises of functional, non-functional, technical and services, as well as needs and tools that will support project development. Further to, such will help us to locate, and find, as per availability, the equipments needed, in view to prepare and ensure a proper development plan.

THE FUNCTIONAL REQUIREMENTS

Defined prior in the project identification definitions (applications proposal), the following will be reviewed:

Functional requirements:

- Storing maps, pictures, textual information
- Store coordinates, organization details, records
- Browsing/searching/exports/imports and print handling
- Securing information

Storing maps, pictures, textual information

Maps and information, about the country side, the roads that have been collected, will be stored, and retrieved as user clicks the website. As data collections process already been started and 20 photographs have been selected, we now move on to the storage requirements. A storage space, needed to accommodate, and another external device, listed earlier, will record and backup the information, prior to loss. At this stage, storage is around 50 megabytes estimated, but as implementation will follow, and the data collection process is ongoing, we will definitely need more room to accommodate pictures & records. A first, short term estimation, is a 300 Gigabyte storage, with backup features. Listed earlier, an external storage device, will care for providing a copy of the project in case of loss. Already available, the storage capacities, coupled with a strong pc, would be the needy materials at this stage.

Store coordinates, organization details, records

Storing coordinates, organization details, records: a database of information will be created, to host records of organizations that contribute to the making of the tourism industry. Hence, when a user connects to the website, and asks for particular information, he will retrieve any information stored. One of the needs is to build effective an storage retrieval system. Sql, or access as database software, would be appropriate to handling the record types and miscellaneous information.

The reason of choosing Microsoft access, or SQL, as databases, is that they can handle bulk information, and acts rapidly for browsing and searching. Microsoft access is well known, since the eighties to handling and communicating with other software such as excel, web connections very well. SQL on the other hand, has been developed as a robust software, taking care of large tables and organizations. The choice, for databases administration, will be definitively one of them, depending upon accessibility, disks costs at an initial stage.

Browsing, searching and report handling, is one of the most important stage in storing records. Finding out the right information kind, the right places to stay, or to be, is handled by browsing abilities mostly, contributed by a database. So, content viewing must be quick and effective, while delivering user's requests. For that, the web pages will be developed onto html, with some flavours of java and asp.

Another fact is saving the information in a proper way, in a good display format. These small tasks often lead to confusion in users while browsing, and must be aligned all through and with the display output. GPS coordinates, will be loaded, and simple means of uploading onto, will be sought for. Google earth, google maps and other free software will be of help, to support the ideas collected, and will form part of the requirements to provide clean display layouts.

Information security, is yet another important issue, in a internet environment. Promoting pictures, information and safeguarding information are key points in making a website reliable. While a proper backup system ensures secure recovery, live data has to be protected. Antivirus software, password policies are amongst the measures strengthening the privacy and security of data. A first level of requirements definition, can be assembled at this stage, describing the main aspects of the systems supplies.

Service	Hardware	Software
Capture photos	Digital camera	Photo Transfer
Storing maps	Hardisk	Windows
Records handling	Paper/Hardisk	Access/sql
Web designs		Templates
Maps		Google earth
GPS converts		free utilities
Antivirus		Mcafee
Backup		Microsoft

NON FUNCTIONAL & PERFORMANCE REQUIREMENTS

Piror in the PID, the non-functional specifications, defined primarily, is further refined:

- Providing security of information
- Allowing a large quantity of users as well as quick multiprocessing facilities
- Capacity to store large volumes of pictures, maps and text information

Security of information

Securing information, and protecting them, is one of the key requirements, when going online. Merely, with millions of users, a site needs proper security, in view of not to be breached by data protection acts. Security starts from the very first considerations in designing, and ends up in implementation. Once a platform is stable, information can be developed, and grow. These actions, helps a lot to defining and protecting the boundaries of the designing perimeter, makes it safe for browsing, virus free, and viable content available.

Providing security of information:

- Physical access: accessing the IT/server systems. The room is locked, and only authorized persons have the key to accessing it.
- OS/server restrictions: password protection on the pcs, at startup, should give administration rights to authorized personnel.
- Level accessing: levels of access, implies levels of security. The levels of security would be used to provide access to levels of the database, such as modifying, or changing records.

Multiprocessing facilities

Since the website will be available to the public, number of hits, may start slowly, until it reaches a peak point. Through, users may request different types of information, at the same time, and the hardware needs must be aligned to what is needed, accommodating gradually to growth. Here, I would suggest a single processor device, with adequate memory, graphics, so as to kick of the project. Gradually, if the systems' needs increases with time, then moving to a twin processing capability pc, with doubled up memory will become imperative. Defining the multiprocessing hardware needs, we have:

- Single P4 duo core processor
- 2Gb of Ram
- 500 GB storage(with an external disk as backup)
- DVD writer
- 512 Mb graphics card

Along with, we need a 512 kbps adsl line, with a LAN gateway gigabit entry points.

Capacity plans

Gradual monitoring of the disks cost, will provide a clear notion of the increase in storage, and the increase in storage space can accompany the previsions. Sometimes a disk is added into the pc, or raid 5 configured on a server, that enables hot plugging, while the server is running live. On the long term perspective, raid 5 on server, is suitable; but for now I would suggest adding disks manually, as a cost effective and non-critical system.

Summing up the non-functional and performance requirements, we have:

- Physical access
- Os/server restrictions
- Level accessing
- Capacity planning
- Website monitoring

TECHNICAL REQUIREMENTS

Technical requirements, is the nuts and bolts of the system. As it has been a subset in functional and non-functional requirements and describe earlier, we can now get into a detailed list of what we want as technical needs:

Item	Software	Hardware/details
PC		core 2 duo,2 Gb RAM, 500 Gb store
Backup	Microsoft	500 GB external disk
GPS stick	free utilities	Garmin 200, 205
Digital Camera	Windows administration	To transfer pictures
Operating system	Vista/XP	
Document editing	Office 2007 standard	
Map editing	Google earth	
Display Unit		17" LCD
ADSL Line		512 Kbps
Photo Editing	Microsoft/adobe	

USABILITY

Effective usage of the system, is what can be described as the overall usability rating. Providing the right information about backpacking, with a proper display, good information designs, will makes the site an effective and enjoyable experience. Information type, display size, fields are therefore the basic usable characteristics that the system should deliver.

Through the steps in defining the functional requirements and collecting hardware, we have selected the least costly and minimum requirements, commonly known as "thin configurations", so as to incur low expenses, for the project to be up and running. Once the project, is working, and needs growth, the hardware requirements and even software can be upgraded, in view to deliver better performance and a finer product.

REQUIREMENTS COLLECTION PROCESS

Functional

Collecting and gathering data: about roads, hospitals, lodging places, fuelling, and services. Gathering data, is done through contact with stakeholders and written on paper. Later on, the paper documents are converged into electronic form, through input, care of transcripting process. Next is the action, of converting data collected into records. For such GPS, camera, storage devices are the tools that will be used. GPS will be bought, as camera and storage is already available. We hence have all tools needed for the requirements collection process. The last process is how to manipulate data. Manipulating, incorporating information with photos, involves using conversion software like google earth and other freely available software on the internet, or even developed modules, that liase with the different record types. This will be dealt, in the design chapter, later on.

The functional requirements underline the basic steps in gathering data, with simple means to collect and store opinions, pictures, and other information. Better means of data collections, are indeed available, like voice recording, or image recording. But this would consume a lot more resources, at additional costs. Hence, the ideal way, is to stay within a reasonable courseline, and if growth is experience, thus we accommodate more resources to it.

Non-functional

Having as secure measures physical lockups, access levels and password policies, a computer administrator will find all ease in minor security policies.

Multiprocessing & capacity planning, also are within the expected performance specified.

Technical

One of the main aspects of Mauritius is that we intend to grow our IT industry into a cyber island. In view to grow this ideal of computer literacy, hardware vendors are cropping up, in all corners of the island. So, our abilities, to obtain technical equipments and materials, are very much easier, compared to the earlier times. Pcs and hardware will be easy to find. The constraint remains that GPS and software licenses are expensive and not so popular actually. To circumvent such, I have proposed to use freeware as much as possible and buy a garmin GPS 205 series.

REQUIREMENTS COLLECTION PROTOCOLS

The following methods will be used as data collection process, for the project:

- Interviews(phone/face to face)
- Questionnaire
- Onsite record writing(roads GPS etc)

Method justification

Some aspects in the data collection process, will require thorough interviewing, while other filing forms or records, while on route for a particular trip. For instance, collecting information, on a owner's point of view, would require interviewing. Interviews, provides a direct transcript of someone's opinion. Phone interviews, is also an effective method, as sometimes travelling, or meeting owners, may loosen schedules. In view to have owners' ideas expressed, interviews will be the ultimate collection protocol, whereas, road trips and questionnaires will be used to collect static information. Static data, that needs little writing, suites much that method. Places like hospitals, lodgings, and even restaurants require specific data. Restaurants for instance will require the type of food served, the location, contact addresses, needs little fill in, and hence, using a questionnaire for specified cases, is the adequate method, easy and quick fill-in.

Another record gathering will be for routes, going to sightseeing, inland tourism places. On road, we have to collect and write information. For instance, in road track, several GPS points must be observed. In addition to, we may supplement with notes.

The simple mean is, through a GPS device, like the garmin 200 series, record the coordinates, of various points, and log onto a sheet. Additional notes, such as interviews and questionnaires, are to be collected separately, as hand written collection. Once again, the choice goes for easy and simple data collection methods, as it is easier to deal with, and little expenses are incurred. As example of the data collection mentioned, records collected have been placed into the appendix.

Conclusions

Problems encountered:

- ❖ Some part of the data collections require extensive time, as owners absent or not available.
- ❖ Schedules difficult to find, as I work on a full-time basis, and meeting up with the different stake holders, often clashes.
- ❖ To find a proper GPS within the island: At last, the garmin 200 series comes on the market in Mauritius. Very expensive, and it does not have any maps inbuilt for Mauritius. I had to incur the expenses from my own salary, and use it only as a point recorder.
- ❖ Maps treatments into suitable graphical form and rendering, as it is the first time I am working on.

Overcoming the challenges

- ❖ Missing schedules were re-organised into weekends, and catch-up time re-allocated.
- ❖ GPS: garmin 205, bought.
- ❖ Maps rendering: I allocated more time, for better rendering, and used Google earth, as a help.

REQUIREMENTS ANALYSIS

After data gathering, analysing them, into meaningful forms, and providing trends of the needs of the market can be derived.

Analysis & Evaluation of requirements

The simple methods, have collected more than many records, successfully. We are now aiming at converging them into electronic form, with a analytic point of view.

Interviews collected were very positive. Owners liked the idea of the project. They prefer to post their advert or information onto a single place, rather than providing a website for each and everyone. Another point we noted is that Mauritius has a lot of services and businesses for tourists, than expected. The fact is that there is no proper marketing for. The data collection, will comprise of certain parts of the island, at first, the main beaches and places, as a startup. Gradually information, and coordinates will complement the database.

The same process is intended for route plotting. The main roads, the main round about, leading to public and common beaches will be observed first. Coastal roads on the second aim, will be derived so as to form up the route network. Along, records of restaurants, fuel places, and lodgings will be collected, in view to show up, what are the places of interest for a tourist, on the highways and main roads.

Thus the plan, makes a complete data collection process, ongoing though the implementation phase .Data collected must often be reviewed, even after implementation, as new roads, new places pops up and evolves.

Through the chapters defined, discussion of methods, we now sum up, with a complete requirements specification for the project.

Full Requirements specification

Point	Software	Hardware/details
PC		core 2 duo,2 Gb RAM, 500 Gb store
Backup	Microsoft	500 GB external disk
GPS stick	free utilities	Garmin 200,205 series
Digital Camera	Windows administration	To transfer pictures
Operating system	Vista/XP	
Document editing	Office 2007 standard	
Map editing	Google earth	
Display Unit		17" LCD
ADSL Line		512 Kbps
Photo Editing	Microsoft/adobe	
Access restrictions	Windows/sql administration	Physical lockup
Capacity storage plan		Extensible drives
Website Monitoring	Utilities	

SUMMARY

Throughout, requirements definition, gathering and defining, the list becomes clearer, and trying to gather the required resources becomes a fairly easy process. The difficulties mentioned, will be tackled with additional time resources, and efforts, in view to get a nice project afterwards.

As compacted, the required equipments lists have been collected within basic aims: the thinnest configuration possible, for the system to be up and running. Thinnest, implies, the less costs, yet effective items, that is available on the local market. The list, is complete, as most needs for designing has been mentioned, but in events of unseen design needs, one or two items, may contribute to finalising the above list.

CHAPTER 4

DESIGN

OVERVIEW

The design phase of this project is to present, a new façade of web, to surfers. Through simple means, and yet less costly materials and equipments, design will shape the project, as expected by the aims and objectives to be met, that was initially defined.   Classifying information, in order to present it to the stakeholders, is one of the pillar steps, in design. Routes plans, Lodging and food, sight seeing places, need all to be collected, and represented in a proper way.

Instances of the web layout, would be primarily, a mere representation of our island, and of the services we offer. Services include a brief of our country, and maps, layouts that can help any user to travel around the island. Further on, points will be shown, for lodging, restaurants, and hospitals and other services as well. All these will be amongst the popular web pages, and along, a blog spot, or forum for sharing of views. Although the most prominent, information treat, will be the handling of maps, geography and tracing routes, with GPS coordinates. This done, a means will be derived for the users, to download routes, maps or layouts, corresponding to respective places around.

Briefing the discussion, we have the following information needs, to work with:

- Introduction of the country: Our economy, stability, infrastructure, technologic abilities, and our people's hospitality.
- Background previews: Pictures of the island
- Statuses: Weather forecasts
- Services: Sports, Shopping, Lodging, Medical, Leisure
- Mapping: maps, route plans, and interesting spots

This gives someone an idea of what kind of country the person will be coming to. Since Mauritius is classified as part of the African continent, few ressembles us in terms of political stability and development. Further to, we have a tropical island's flavored beaches with inland natural beauty. The notes make a plus, towards the preferred destinations of foreigners.

OVERALL DESIGN

The overall design, will be a blend of providing all the mentioned information, through fluid a plan, whereby accessing information, and displaying, is to be developped. The development, will be modular, each module developed independently and interated afterwards. Along, inter connection of modules, data transfers, will be designated for a smoother overall completeness. As a starting point, the main aspects that will make the website, are as follows:

- Introduction of our country, and the various aspects that makes us a modern paradise
- General information, weather, recommendations
- Maps, and geography, places of fuelling, care and restaurants
- Database of records, retrieved & updated from web
- Adverts, forums and contact information

Arranging the information in particular ways, enhancing data communications between the different modules, is yet to be build. With the help of modular design, and the three steps such as component, data and interface, we will go through the designing face, in view to promote a better plan for implementation. Looking deeper into the overall design, we have:

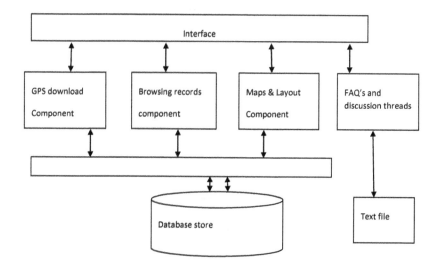

As from the schema above, the following major components, will make sure the entire system is running:

- GPS download component: GPS points, on each particular route, can be downloaded onto local resources of user's pc or mobile device
- Browsing records component: Browsing/updation of records & places
- Maps, layout component & gallery: Display of maps, layers & pictures
- Links/forum threads: Links to interesting sites/discussions notes of any users

SEQUENCE DIAGRAMS

The sequences of flow, of input information, to the system and that returns back, has to be designed and properly sorted, so as to eliminate redundancies at start, and enhance the fluid flow of information within the project. Sequence diagrams help a lot, to understand how working modules interact altogether, to produce a viable system. Let us draw the intended diagrams, for each module defined:

The main inputs:

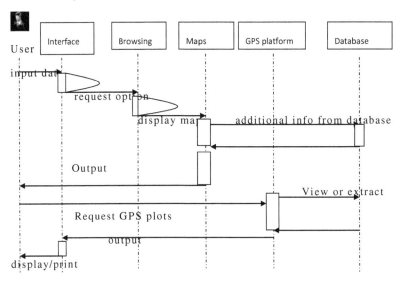

Browsing Module

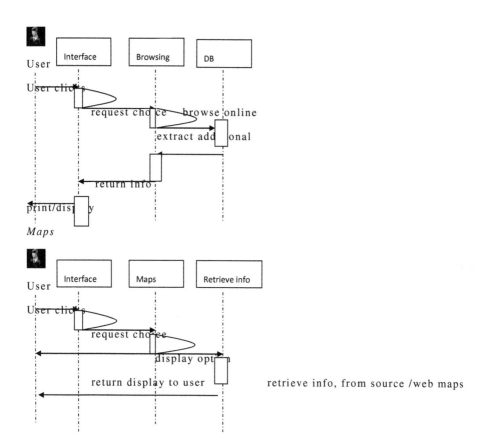

Maps

retrieve info, from source /web maps

GPS

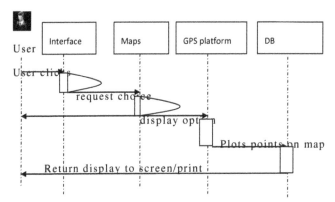

FAQ/FORUM

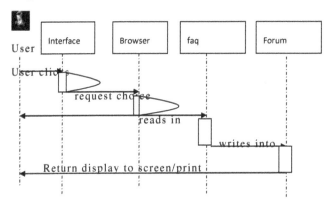

COMPONENT DESIGN

As the overall design generates an intergrated idea of how the finished prouct will look like, component design goes into deeper details, of how the system will interact altogether. Basic building skills have been devised, as "light" and easy interconnection between components. An intent to, favorise a performant system and efficiency in treating and handling information.

Read/write components of the interface design

Interface design basically acts between the user's guidance and amongst the coding, and information store. Easy process going, it fetches user's request, loads maps, or information onto database. Here the minimum component usage, shows efficient reactions and process time in between, as shown in the figure below:

ACTIVITY SPECIFICATION

The interface component acts between the user or operator, in view to navigate through the website. It reacts to clicks mostly, then directs loading of pages on screen. Interface component, has most basic sub-components within the component design process, showing each step that an action is taken to load, refresh a page.

COMPONENT SPECIFICATION

Read component: read/capture input from user

Buffers: keep in store choices of user

DB component: interaction with the database

Display component: displays output on screen/print, and loads applets if needy.

Maps

Maps acts on the interface component, and loads the mapping information interactively. First, the geography of the island, and afterwards, data that comes onto it. In between there is user reaction to processes, and retrieving from the database, with ability to display and print:

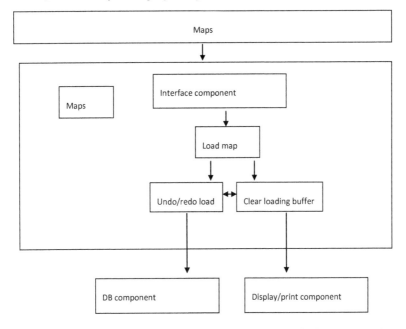

Activity specification

The maps component design, illustrate the concept of showing maps of the island, either in layers, or parts of it enlarged, with the ideal information a backpacker wants. Merely, it accepts user's choices, and through the store, loads the maps with information such as GPS, or other points like lodging, restaurants and fuel places.

From an operator's point of view, maps will be added, directly onto a web template, modify when necessary, in view to provide users new taste and places to visit in Mauritius. Thus maintenance steps and activities within may differ.

Map activities, will be the main aspects of the design, an activity that will put forward new horizons for the web user.

Component specification

Interface component: The interface components ensure proper interaction between system and user.

- Load map components: loading and refreshing of maps and layouts
- DB component: interaction with the database
- Display component: displays output on screen/print, and loads applets if needy.

GPS component

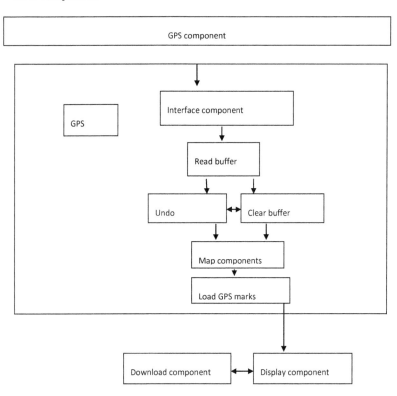

Activity specification

The GPS component, loads information onto the map components, and provides user displays of where he is, and where to go. Moreover, it will help user to download, the course line on any mobile device, or locally onto a pc. Here user can choose which routes he wants to, and load onto his GPS module, to travel around.

Component specification

The new components are hence defined:

- Maps: loading of the map component
- Buffering: loading user inputs and validation
- Load GPS: this component loads the GPS marks, of the routes along the map
- Download: GPS plots can be downloaded onto local pc, or mobile devices.

CONCLUSION

The design components have been written, as per steps defined primarily in chapters 2 & 3. Methods of components derived, as well as schema's and diagram such as entity relationship and sequence diagrams helps to conceiving the final product better, and how it works, in the inside. Moreover, the tasks of designing components being broken into simple parts, a perspective of how the implementation would be, can already be imagined, at this stage.

DATA DESIGN

We need now, to elaborate on data requirements, which will provide a complete sense, complementing the component design of the system. A detailed data structure can be designed through an entity relationship diagram, showing the entity and information interaction within the system.

EER diagram

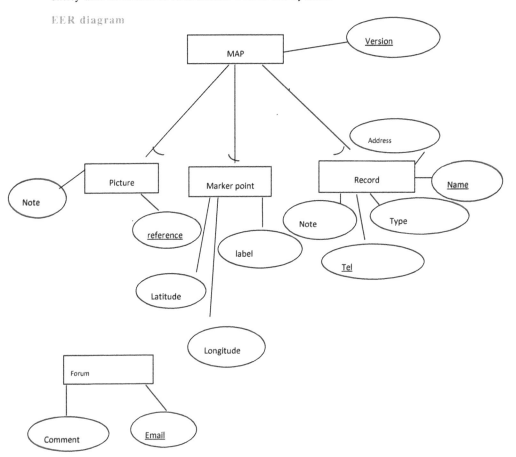

The ER diagram, is aimed to show the interaction and relationship between the different classes, and fields to be implemented. Here, a map, has many marker points, where each could represent a specific location. Each of which has their own field, key fields assigned in underlined. Forum is not related to the overall table, as it is static information, with incrementing fields only.

The ER diagram is based upon the actual design plan, and if minor changes occur, then ER will need to reflec those. Hence diagrams are not final, and may subsequently undergo minor changes during implementation phases, as performance enhancements may be considered.

INTERFACE DESIGN

The world wide web has many sites concerning tourism in Mauritius, as viewed and analysed earlier in chapters one and two, many sites offer different perspectives of Mauritian culture, and environment. Each has a different flavour of presenting to users, and with that scope, the interface design, will be oriented to the specific needs of project, delivering a new may to plan holidays, as easily clickable, to the users.

< The description of Mauritius, as an island, with favourable environments for tourists and back pakers. A background image will be inserted, for a lively display. The description will accompany some proofs of our preferences, from foreigners-that is the yearly statistics; and about our safe environments. >	
	< This space will be intended, as an overview of our different sectors
Table of contents	Of our economy, and show our stability. Pop up screens, will show showing the different axles that makes us an attractive island for
	Tourists. Main overviews will show, the technologic trends,
Overview	Infrastructure, economy, business, and some other major sectors.
MAPS	
GPS & Routes	
Information	
Forum & FAQs	
Contact us	
Gallery Links weather Airliners	

Overall, the first impression, the interface will be clickable parts, to navigation. The table of content, defines the map, and whereabouts of the website, linking to the other pages.

Most part, is static information. The gallery, will be a showcase, of images, where user clicks to enlarge, view previous, and forward options. Links such as weather conditions and airliners, brings users, to other sites, as complementary resources.

MAPS

< The geography of the island. A brief of our geography, with facts and figures, and pictures. >

MAP

GPS & routes

Information

Forum & FAQs

Database admin

Contact us

<this area will show the main map, with the corresponding geography of the island, the mountain areas, rivers and lakes. Upon click, other map layouts will be loaded, such as location of services, sightseeing places and beaches, as well as miscellaneous informations.>

Picture showcase

GPS and routes

<GPS and routes, will cover mainly the different GPS plots sets, of routes, sightseeing, cities and important places around the island. Upon clicks, user can save routes, plot points or print.>

TABLE OF CONTENTS

MAPS

Gps & ROUTES

FORUM & FAQs'

DATABASE ADMIN

CONTACT US

<Pop up and upload point, Routes>

<Pop up and upload point, cities>

<Pop up and upload point, places>

Save route　　　　　　Save GPS points　　　　Print

Information

the section provides an information-based page, whereas contacts of services, business types, and miscellaneous information would be available>

TABLE OF CONTENTS

MAPS

GPS & ROUTES

FORUM & FAQS'

DATABASE ADMIN

CONTACT US

Service type:

<Display: Service Name>

<Display: Address>

<Display: Contact information>

<Display: General information>

SUMMARY

The chapter has underlined important aspects of design, and demonstrate the approaches into rendering better implementation of the project. Parts of component designing, interface designing have been covered, showing in detail, the interaction of processes. The methods that have been used, are popular ones, that adheres to a touch of simplicity. It is good to note, however that the design may undergo slight changes during the implementation phase, so as to render a better quality product and enhancing performance. Along, we move to the chapter 5, implementing the design concepts.

CHAPTER 5

SYSTEM IMPLEMENTATION

OVERVIEW

This chapter, will go through the different phases of implementation, as defined previously, in the design chapter. The steps such as component design, data design and interface design, will be taken into account, into developing the system of project. Implementation on the overall, will be summed, as an instance, of how the design was turned into reality, with the steps, facilities and issues encountered. Prior to the three pillars of design, there are key resources, that have been used, throughout the implementation process, and a flavour of the key aspects, which will be described further below:

Tools

The selected tools for implementation: GPS, pc, adsl connection to web, office software, access database, google earth & maps and developing languages. Languages include javascript, html, asp, and few php, for client server computing. These blend, will be of usage to building the implementation. Considering the different language flavours, mixing them into favourable webpages, and connecting them altogether, will need time and skilful development. Moreover, in aid to, the author has the opportunity to learn about, through the internet itself, as the web offers great places of instructing programmers(ex: www.w3schools.com). Templates also are available, as well as other paid services, as prior to web development. But these will be left aside, as it will resume in a rise in costing, Moreover, developing on one's own, makes skills grow, as well as the abitity to track down errors and correct more easily. The basic tools mentioned, we proceed further to see how the application is build.

APPLICATION BUILD

The application build is in phases. Firstly, it will be representing information onto web, using html, and google maps. Second is the interaction of the database, which will be done through asp and XML language. And first, reading from files, and loading points on screen. Lets have an indepth look, of how the application building would be done. Html, the hypertext markup language, the very starting point of internet develop, is one of the simplest ways of representing basic interfaces. Generators such as frontpage, publishing are now available to "prepare" an html page. As colors, photos can be used onto, the main interfaces will be prepared with, such as the main page, links and backgrounds. An html page, can comprise of asp, php, or java parts. Thus ASP, will be used to connect to an asp database, reading the information inside, and pulling out the necessary ones, to be projected further on. PHP on the other hand, will be used to perform any web to local activities, such as pulling information from GPS readings, or pushing onto the same devices. Finally, output, will be done, either on google earth or maps, as google has already detailed format representations of the island.

I tried one or two samples of the different languages available and google mash mashups. This so, In view to have a picture, on what shall be needed, and what needs to be done, to deliver expected products, in a timely and proper way. The first impression of having a diverse collection of languages for system development was gradually confirmed. The web, is mostly a developed platform comprising of applets, different languages, accessings and other flavours as well. Java scripts being for computing on the clients side, asp being to interact with databases, php server side, and html, to coding a graphical user interface will be the basic developing tools. The languages are mostly free of charge, very few flavours and utilities being sold, we will try to focus on a development that is of no cost, along with the project. Coding templates used, will be of public licenses, stated in comments, in the code part, or function. Such action is to provide a better rendering of the website and functions. For instance using a flash template, would be the ideal tool, to render a page, or a collection of pictures. Lastly, google maps for developers, will be a facility to represent Mauritius and GPS data on web form. Google maps development, have undergone considerable change these last periods. Google maps, offers, source development codes, that can be changed to one's suiting, with API(Application Programming Interface), that each has to freely register. An insight of the steps of building:

The mixture of developing languages and applications is such, as to favorise better component connection, and interfacing. An insight of the development would be: mashup to read points from a database store which caters for relating information, records basically. Another option, will be reading of a GPS, and plotting the points to display or even downloading routes displayed. The entire information, represented onto an html/asp/php interfacing.

Before, getting into component implementation, it is important note that: the build should be supported into asp enabled website host and viewed through modern browsers, supporting cookies, java and asp interactions.

COMPONENT IMPLEMENTATION

The component implementation was a difficult, part as it meant communication in between the interfaces and the databases, and user responses. As it is essential to the good functioning of the project, much time was allocated to finding the right means to communicate between modules, and fluidise movement of information in between them. The internet, as an online source of reading, was adequate in resources, for this process. The basic bolts of component implementation, are:

- Reading from users, and displaying on internet.
- Reading from database, and displaying on maps.
- Reading and writing files, and display on maps, that is the GPS component.

The three points mentioned, will be tackled in XML form. For instance, while reading from the database, an XML file is created, that can be considered as a platform, which is afterwards uploaded, onto maps. Another part, will be, uploading a GPS file, converting it into a readable form, and hence, pass it onto a map, to be displayed. XML pays much contribution to these tasks, as it is much flexible writing and provides fluid transfers of fields.

Maps, databases, and interfacing.

Representing maps, through google mashups, is the ideal way to smartly presenting points and places of interests. An alternative method, was to prepare a map, through GIS or scans, and plot corresponding points as layers on. As a result, the method would have required extensive treatments of maps, and plotting of points. Futher to, the rendering, would not have been as practical, as displaying it on web. Hence, google maps, was the best choice, as it offered the same services, openly to developers. Public source codes are available, and it can be customised, and merged into asp pages, as well as java scripting. For the mapping process, I used google maps, that can upload points from an XMl template, that in turn, is pumped from an access database. Most practical though, but tricky in programming due to different language interactions, the result became a nice page, where spots of interesting places are loaded:

Welcome to the maps page.

This part, shows points uploaded, from a database. Our administrator updates regularly interesting spots to see.
    At this stage only a few togglers are available: Hotels around the coastal regions
                                           : Fuelling places(caltex stations)
                                           : Restaurants
                                           : Hospitals

Instructions:
Click on Show labels to view labelling
Toggle Hotels, Fuelling, Restaurants, if you wish to see only a category
Click on the spots, to get more information(eg:location of spot)
Left click on mouse, to drag around & double-click to get more details

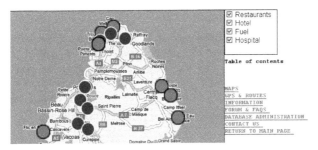

This map previews coloured spots, fetched from database, via XML, of restaurants, hotels, hospitals and fuel places. The spots are merely records of name, latitude, longitude. In addition to, clicking on a particular spot, details such as address & location is displayed. The basic information provided, can be amended into providing more: telephone numbers and emails, through labels, or side by side display of what the database has.

Easily clickable, precise output to users, with a smart presentation, hides the different component accessing in the background.

A preview of the coding:

AccesstoXML file(font reduced to 8, code in appendix)

<%

'=== declare variables

Dim objConn, strConnect, strSQL, rs, tb, mdbFile, objFSO, xmlFile, objWrite

'=== filename variables

```
xmlFile = Server.MapPath("markerdata.xml")
mdbFile = Server.MapPath("gpsdatabase.mdb")


'=== tab character for xml file
tb = chr(9)
'=== instantiate objects
set objFSO = Server.CreateObject( "Scripting.FileSystemObject" )
Set objConn = Server.CreateObject( "ADODB.Connection" )
'=== connect to database
objConn.Open "Provider=Microsoft.Jet.OLEDB.4.0;Data Source=" & mdbFile
'=== open/create xml file
If Not objFSO.FileExists( xmlFile ) Then objFSO.CreateTextFile( xmlFile )
set objWrite = objFSO.OpenTextFile( xmlFile, 2 )
'=== open the xml file
objWrite.WriteLine("<?xml version=""1.0"" encoding=""ISO-8859-1""?>")
objWrite.WriteLine("<marker>")
strSQL = "SELECT * FROM records"
Set rs = objConn.Execute(StrSQL)
'=== loop through results
Do While not rs.EOF
objWrite.Write(tb & tb & "<marker name='" & rs("name") & "'" )
objWrite.Write(tb & tb & " <address>" & rs("address") & "</address>")
objWrite.Write(tb & tb & " <tel>" & rs("tel") & "</tel>")
objWrite.Write(tb & tb & " <lat>" & rs("lat") & "</lat>")
objWrite.Write(tb & tb & " <lng>" & rs("lng") & "</lng>")
objWrite.Write(tb & tb & " <type>" & rs("type") & "</type>")
```

```
objWrite.Write(tb & tb & "  <region>" & rs("region") & "</region>")

                    objWrite.WriteLine("")

                         rs.MoveNext

                            Loop

                '=== finish xml file

             objWrite.WriteLine("</marker>")

                     objWrite.Close()

                          %>
```

The XML file

<markers>

<marker name="Chez Patrick" address="Royal Road, Mahebourg" lat="-20.411891" lng="57.706032" type="restaurant" />

GPS to maps

With the same practical methodologies, another aspect in coding the GPS functionalities and interactions is ready to be implemented. A google map, is used to deliver or provide information to GPS, while user can upload his GPS file, for reading. In that case, user loads a file(GPX for garmin type GPS), the file is then turned into text, and read to an XML one. The XML file, then returns values(latitude and longitude to a mashup). Here, mashup reads and edits my locations, and through points clicked, users can prepare his/her route, and download again onto the GPS. For that, user, can click on show points in XML, which is read into a text file, and added into the GPX. Such an instance, gives way to preparing planned routes, and feeding into GPS modules, a preview shown below:

GPS and Routes

This pages shows the different routes that you may opt, to go to a specific place
Instructions

Click on any place, on the spot, and click several points, on the route, you may opt to destination
On end of route, click, closing point
Click clear to restart again
Undo last: for removing the last point plotted
Show points txt will load a text file, showing the GPS points plotted
Show points xml, will load an xml file, showing the GPS points plotted
Click to upload: prompts uploading of GPS file, & returns your location from GPS

File Name: [　　　　　　] Browse...

[SUBMIT]　[Load point]

If the intial point is in port louis, and user wants to go to Quatres Bornes: On a series of clicks, polylines are plotted, as well as the corresponding GPS points on the right hand side of the map. User can also see the total distance, and printing. Behind the component interaction is observed:

Upload GPX file → convert to Text file → Load to XML→ Google map, fetches in, displays.

Google maps export to text /XML → injects into text file & convert into GPX→user loads into GPS

Extract of coding:

The GPS load module(font-8)

```
<html>

<body>

<p>GPS read module:</p>

<%

Dim x

xmlFile = Server.MapPath("markerdata.txt")

Set fs=Server.CreateObject("Scripting.FileSystemObject")
```

'rename file uploaded

fso.MoveFile "GPX.gpx",
"c:\MemberSites\MemberSites_AspSpider_Ws\universityproject\database\gpx.txt"

set fso = Nothing

set objFSO = Server.CreateObject("Scripting.FileSystemObject")

If Not objFSO.FileExists(xmlFile) Then objFSO.CreateTextFile(xmlFile)

set objWrite = objFSO.OpenTextFile(xmlFile, 2)

objWrite.WriteLine("<?xml version=""1.0"" encoding=""ISO-8859-1""?>")

objWrite.WriteLine("<marker>")

x=0;

Do while EOF

x=x+1;

Set f=fs.OpenTextFile(Server.MapPath("gpx.txt"), "x")

if (f.ReadLine)= ("lat")

then

objWrite.WriteLine(tb & "<point>")

objWrite.WriteLine(tb & tb & "<lat>" & rs("latin") & "</lat>")

objWrite.WriteLine(tb & "</point>")

else

if (f.ReadLine)= ("lng")

then

objWrite.WriteLine(tb & "<point>")

objWrite.WriteLine(tb & tb & "<lng>" & rs("lng") & "</lng>")

objWrite.WriteLine(tb & "</point>")

Wend

f.Close

Set f=Nothing

Set fs=Nothing

fso.MoveFile "markerdata.txt",
"c:\MemberSites\MemberSites_AspSpider_Ws\universityproject\database\markerda
ta.xml"

set fso = Nothing

%>

</body>

</html>

Map

Addroute:

```
function addRoutePoint(point) {

var dist = 0;

if (!routePoints[lineIx]) {

routePoints[lineIx] = Array();

routeMarkers[lineIx] = Array();

}

routePoints[lineIx].push(point);

if (routePoints[lineIx].length > 1)   {

plotRoute();

dist = routePoints[lineIx][routePoints[lineIx].length-2].distanceFrom(point) /
1000;

totalDistance += dist;

document.getElementById("dist").innerHTML = 'Total Distance: '+
totalDistance.toFixed(3) + ' km';

}

else {
```

```
        routeMarkers[lineIx][routePoints[lineIx].length-1] = new
           GMarker(point,{icon:greenIcon,title:'Start'});

     map.addOverlay(routeMarkers[lineIx][routePoints[lineIx].length-1]);

}      document.getElementById("route").innerHTML += point.y.toFixed(6) + ' ' +
        point.x.toFixed(6) + ' : ' + dist.toFixed(3) +"<br>";

                                    }
```

DATABASE IMPLEMENTATION

Database implementation, preparing tables, and fields to be stored, is quicker task than building the programming block. A smaller slot of time, is allocated, as table building is a straightforward process. Initially, the author had the choice of either sql, or access as database store. Access 2003 will be favored, as licensing is already available, and because of familiarity. Easy creation of fields & validations are the prior characteristics of the particular choice. Nevertheless, sql is more robust, for database storage and can handle large amounts of data efficiently, fact proven by enterprises worldwide. In that particular project, the author finds unnecessary at this stage to cater for sql storage, as the pilot system, will handle smaller to medium amounts of data.

The tables designed

Forum table

Entity Name	FORUM				
Table Name	Forum				
Description	stores email and notes from users				
Primary Key					
Foreign Key					
References					
Column Name	Data Type	Length	Range	Description	Null?
Email	Text	30		Email type	No
Notes	Text	100		text input, any notes written	No

Pictures

Entity Name	PICTURE					
Table Name	Pictures					
Description	stores information about pictures					
Primary Key	Reference					
Foreign Key						
References						
Column Name	Data Type	Length	Range	Description		Null?
Reference	Autonumber	30		Autonumber generated		No
Lat	Number	10		Latitude point of shot		No
Lng	number	10		longitude		No
Notes	Text	100		Accompanying notes		

Records

Entity Name	RECORD				
Table Name	Records				
Description	Stores records of businesses, services of the organization				
Primary Key	Name				
Foreign Key					
References					
Column Name	Data Type	Length	Range	Description	Null?
Name	Text	30		Business name	No
Address	Text	50		Company/service address	No
Lat	Number	10		Latitude	No
Lng	Number	10		Longitude	No
Type	Text	10		Restaurant/hotel/fuel...	No

Routes

Entity Name	ROUTE					
Table Name	Routes					
Description	Information about routes					
Primary Key	Reference					
Foreign Key						
References						
Column Name	Data Type	Length	Range	Description		Null?
Reference	Number	10		Autonumber		No
Notes	Text	100		text input, any notes written		No
Lat1	Number	10		Latitude		No
Lng1	Number	10		Longitude		No
Lat2	Number	10		Latitude		No
Lng 2	Number	10		Longitude		No

INTERFACE IMPLEMENTATION

Interface communicates to users. The very first impression a user gets, is through loading the interface. Hence, interfaces must be meaningful, simple and smart enough to provide and support what a user needs. In that particular reason, HTML is the right language for providing static text and picture-based information. In addition to, javascripting, and flash, may be added into, so as to flavour slideshows as well as other interesting information. Backgrounds, links and slideshows, will be part of html implementing, as it loads fast and helps to provide clear, simple interface displays:

The main interface

Uopproject.html

Information

In addition to, information treats, input/updates and browsing, asp will be part of the html coding. Asp provides connection to the database, querying tables, and formatting back for user viewing. Forms to capture, asp connection strings to access the database, with validation and security procedures, are as follows:

Administrator access

Username and login, is retrieved and compared from the database, and validates

User: [   ]
Password: [   ]
[Login]

administrator access.

Any user can browse records:

1	Chez Patrick	Royal Road Mahebourg
2	Choice food palace	Royal road phoenix
3	Club mediteranee	Royal road, pointe aux cannoniers
4	Debonnairs pizza	Intendence St Port Louis
5	Domaine des pailles	Pailles

Prev Page	Next Page
pagelist 1 2 3 4 5	

Table of contents: MAPS GPS & ROUTES INFORMATION FORUM & FAQS DATABASE ADMINISTRATION CONTACT US RETURN TO MAIN I

Gallery

The gallery, is a slideshow of pictures, collected from various sites and labelled. It is sought along, to couple the album, or albums, with a table, whereby latitudes and longitunal information can be provided to the user.

IMPLEMENTATION FEEDBACK

Integrating all the implementation altogether, has been a tedious experience, as a variety of developing tools has been used. From ASP programming, connection to databases, sql statements, to mashups modifications, passing through java scripting and php uploading and downloading, the development has been long to be derived. The author, used IIS, that is local based loading for asp connections and html constructs, before preparing the final pilot system.

Component implementation, were done with XML mostly. The latter being a very flexible platform, getting inside access databases, through text files, it has been an excellent "joker" to achieving integrity in component implementation. Though the final rendering and appearance, author has spent more time than planned on implementation phase. This due to several issues arising:

A common familiar, model of GPS was bought by author, to understand how information saved into it, could be rendered onto points, in a website.   The instance, was rather tedious, as plotting of routes were first done, and afterwards, several means and methods of accessing the written files, were tried.

Plots in GPS observed, represented a large deflection on Google maps. Author has notified google maps of the problem, and once google, correct the deflections, the project will gain in precision in latitude and longitude, without any major change in coding.

The experience acquired, on all aspects was rather enjoying, as it now opens new areas for using such a project. The social impact, targets and addressing will be further broadened in the evaluation and appraisals chapters.

CHAPTER 6

SYSTEM TESTING

The testing phase ensures that the systems' functionalities are delivered to what has been expected, and corners the wrong input and processing types. Testing activities observed, forming part of the test plan, showing the relative conformity to the design and implementation objectives. Also, the system testing, will show inconsistencies to be corrected, in view to provide an integral working system. This chapter will deal thoroughly with testing methods, and cases.

THE TESTING STRATEGY

In view to find out the errors, and what corrections need to be done, a testing strategy is imperative. Tests strategies, occurs when the most is tested withing a developed system. In the particular project, test plan will ensure that most functional areas are working to satisfaction, and to the expectations of the user. Moreover, the test plan will cover areas such as verification of the right input types, and validates entries into the database. Since the pilot development, is small, an effective test plan will comprise of: black box tests, and white box tests. In order, to summarise, integrity test, will hence confirm the overall completeness and working condition of the web development. In brief, White box testing will tests modules internal cycles and consider outputs, whereas blackbox testing, will test both inputs and outputs received. afterwards, integrity tests will be done to perceive any mistakes in logic, and make sure that they work altogether, as a single system.

The test plan, will include all modules developed, with tests feeds, expected results and finally, indicate if the tests are successful. In exceptions, the failure, cause and actions to be taken, will be described, in order to further correct the errors and improve from the testing phase.

TEST CASES-EXTRACTS

The test cases developed, testing boundary limits of inputs, and what needs to be validated and verified, lies below. Only certain parts is listed, as the full tests are annexed in appendix 4. B series accounts to Black Blox tests, W for the White Box testing, and finally I for integrity tests.

An extract of the test cases, as a full test plan, lies in the appendix 4.

Test segment	Ref	Test module	Input range	Objective	Expected results	Test priority
Black box	B1	Main interface load	web address	load main page on internet	Loads within secs	High
	B2	Click for sub pages	Clicks	links to maps, gps, information and forum	Browse different pages	High
	B3	Maps page	Clicks	Toggle options-hotels	Hide/view	Medium
	B4	Maps page	Clicks	Toggle options-restaurants	Hide/view	Medium
	B5	Maps page	Clicks	Toggle options-sight seeing	Hide/view	Medium
White box	W1	Database	add record	check if exists in database	Record available	High
	W2	Database	delete record	check if exists in database	Record not available	High
	W3	Database	add record	check if displayed on map	Record available	High
	W4	Database	delete record	check if displayed on map	Record not available	High
Integrity	I 1	Surfing	Clicks	check if all pages can be accessed	Should display all sub pages	High
	I2	Database	Input	check if added record are displayed	Should display record	High
		Database	Clicks	Checks if deled records are displayed	Should not display record	High

Each module tested independently, works fine, as concerned for the integrity tests.

Test gment	Ref	Test module	Input range	Expected results	Actual results	Status
ack x	B1	Main interface load	web address	Loads within secs	As expected	Success
	B2	Click for sub pages	Clicks	Browse different pages	As expected	Success
	B3	Maps page	Clicks	Hide/view	option is hidden/viewed on toggle	Success
	B4	Maps page	Clicks	Hide/view	option is hidden/viewed on toggle	Success
	B5	Maps page	Clicks	Hide/view	option is hidden/viewed on toggle	Success
hite x	W1	Database	add record	Record available	Record found in database	Success
	W2	Database	delete record	Record not available	Record not found in database	Success
	W3	Database	add record	Record available	Record found in database	Success
	W4	Database	delete record	Record not available	Record not found in database	Success
	W5	GPS	Load	Point displayed	Point loaded on screen	Success
egrity	I 1	Surfing	Clicks	Should display all sub pages	As expected	Success
	I2	Database	Input	Should display record	As expected	Success
		Database	Clicks	Should not display record	As expected	Success

IMPLEMENTATION PLAN

GPS and backpakers website, is a pilot projet, in view to find out the future possibilities of programming and using GPS in Mauritius. The basic functions of the project, is working, as per prior tests cases and results revealed, the site is ready to be uploaded. Although the project has achieved a satisfactory level of completeness, more efforts can contribute to building better options websites, facilities to holiday packers coming to Mauritius. For instance, pictures, tags, or movies can also be added onto, or even a local marketplace, where commerce can be practised. At this stage, the pilot web site, is at a good functional and satisfactory level, and ready to be uploaded, following a brief implementation plan, as follows:

- Site installation: Upload on a host
  - o Feed in data
- Implementation & security: Further testing and amendments
  - o Security
  - o Backup
- User installation & monitoring   Needs of browsers
  - o Brief on how to use
  - o Maintenance & statistics

Site installation

As the website has been made with different languages, it is important to load the site, onto a host, that is capable of handling all the options and pages coded. For instance, the host must be able to run asp, php, javascripting, as primary requirements. Some offer free hosting, such as www.somee.com, and it is the one of the ideal place to upload the website developped.

Once loaded, minor corrections are to be done, based upon the test plans and results, as it will provide an enhanced, complete version. Minor corrections will include, pathways to access the database, which will be stored next to the pages, and API codes, from google maps.

An instance of the website, can be viewed at:

http://aspspider.ws/universityproject/uopproject.html

whereby the database administration access, are:

username: admin

password: 1234

username: yasir

password: 091077

*if site is not available, or any questions, i would be glad to reply to you, from my email address: cheers@intnet.mu

Security

Further to minor changes, markers' locations will be updated, as well as pictures and slideshows. Along, the login and password table, will cater for the necessary administrative rights to accessing & updating records.

Coming to security, periodic backups will be observed, once online. A spare, external hardisk will be available for the task, and cuteftp is best to access the hosting place for backup procedures. A script can also be written to access in the host, copy all the pages and databases, into local. This will be dealt in future, as when considering a full system build. Additional security measures will be regular password changes, as well as password policy on local computer, where backup is stored. The local storage place, will be kept in a closed compartment, where only one person has access to.

User installations & monitoring

On different computers, one can check accessing the website, with the different browsers available. The latest version of internet explorer works fine with asp pages, and scripts; the same has been observed with firefox, version 3.X. Hence, if a user has versions below those mentioned, he is kindly advised to look for upgrades.

Each page, will accompany a short note, instructions on how to operate. For example the GPS download module, when click, will instruct user, how to upload his GPX file, while the site will care of the rest. Also, any users, may reply or mail back, in need for additional information.

Overall system maintenance, over regular periods may help to clean up and keep the site fresh, as per user demands.

SUMMARY

Tests conclude into positive results, as well as the integration of the pilot project was done, without major modifications or change in design or development. Although there is, areas of improvement, such as GPS downloading, uploading, or prepared routes to sightseeing. Interesting spots in Mauritius, can also be developed further, so as to provide strategic locations such as schools, fire & police stations. Forums can help to discuss about interesting contacts and other services that the country offers.

Such improvements can be considered after, while building a full & complete system, tailored to the needs of an enterprise or social organisation in Mauritius. Many different perspectives offers can be proposed, from the pilot system developed, part of which will be discussed next in the evaluation and conclusion chapters respectively.

CHAPTER 7

EVALUATION

As the project is coming to end, it is important to evaluate the progress line, achievements made, and areas of interests and impacts. Through this stage, evaluation of the project, will be mainly, how it was produced, compared to the initial aims, and the improvements, conclusions that can be derived on.

PROJECT OUTCOME

The project report, is one testimonial of the steps taken to drive, project to endnote, and second is the pilot website produced. First the report, which describes the analysis, design and development stages, contributes to the problems, challenges and facilities while treating the particular subject-GPS with maps on web. The detailed document, shows how the proposed system, was made, while each step thought, has been realised, or crossed by. In view to evaluate better, let us compare the intial Project Identification Guideline, to the actual product, that is the project report and website.

Initially, the PID was defined with *"Aim is to make use of suitable technologies, to create a "website with mapping layers of the country's routes, places of interest, and corresponding geometry. The web layout will be an instructive material, to backpackers and travelers and even inland sight seers. "*

Considering the aim, it can be further summarized as follows:

- ✓ **Use of suitable technologies for development**
- ✓ **Website, with mapping layers of routes, places of interest**
- ✓ **Instructive material to backpackers and travellers**

✓ Usage of suitable technologies

Technologies involved, were prior to cost, as it was all incurred by the author. As a matter of fact, the tools mentioned in the PID, such as pc, web connection, free developing languages such as VB scripting, ASP, PHP, HTML, XML were widely used. As the web itself was a resourceful place of tutorials, the development, took place, without any other knowledge resources. Although tedious at times, coding was somewhat tricky, while mixing up html forms, ASP, and XML for instance. Time slot was longer than expected, nevertheless, no other expenses were incurred by the author. Resources were optimized, and aim fully met.

✓ Website, with mapping layers of routes, places of interest

Maps of the country, earlier planned to be digitized, was overcome by google maps being open to the public. The latter, being precise, with latitudes and longitudes, and routes, opened its coding to the public, once one has a host and an API. Hence, the process was easier dealt, as maps can now be added with information. Here, the author used markers, to load points of interests from database, route plots through polylines, and uploading from a GPS. The aim, has been successfully met, though refining of codes and component can provide a better render in presentation. Another issue, would be to develop side interests for particulars, such as predevelopped routes, fire and police stations.

✓ Instructive material to backpackers and travelers

The overall project is interesting. Any person coming to Mauritius, can go to the website, view the interesting places, and find the corresponding addresses. In addition to, they can plot their routes, print, and evaluate the different paths or distance to travel. Partially attained, as aim, because the developed product can be improved further: Pictures and tags, can be placed onto, real time GPS catching, or loading from cellular phones. These would services, the author can develop, along for a real project.

Further to, we proceed in examining the objectives defined earlier in chapter one, while proceeding writing of the report:

- **Chapter Two: Introduction of middle class tourism in Mauritius, gathering information, competitors, products, tools and summary**
- **Chapter Three: defining requirements & services, needs, tools. Hence, proceeding to selection of required, evaluation, drafting on the full requirements specification, and summary**
- **Chapter Four: design objectives**
- **Chapter Five: implementation: creation & assembly of the website, with information store. Refine and revise the working model.**
- **Chapter Six: Provides the test plan, test cases and results.**

Chapter Two:

A brief of the tourism industry was gathered from onsite visits, travels, and gathering information through surveys and records. These compiled in the appendix gave a broader view of the expectations of the stakeholders, as the objectives are met.

Chapter Three:

The list of tools, equipments necessary, as prior to "making use of suitable technologies", we refined and drafted. Lists includes software, hardware, networking as well as other devices, such as GPS and Digital camera. Objectives has been met, with the least incurred cost to development.

Chapter Four:

The design objectives, being to integrate all data collections, and present information to bakcpakers, in a planned manner, prior to implementation, were done. Different steps concluded the objectives, such as ER diagrams, database design, interface designs.

Chapter Five:

The creation of the website, with all coding plans taken from the previous chapter, through usage of languages and tutorials from web, made it all a realizable objective. Each module build to sequence diagramming, refined along and the database produced, as designed makes this stage coherent in objective.

Chapter Six:

Testing was done through a test strategy, ensuring most vital parts of the implementation are working. Although most important tests were done, the system may be error prone. Along with thorough testing, some errors may be discovered, as it is practically impossible to testing all parts of a system, even though a pilot one. This part, objective has been almost met with.

Summary-Project outcome

As most objectives have been successfully met with, there are certain areas that can be improved with the project. More facilities offered to backpakers is one, while a better render of the interfaces would be a second thought. The tedious part, that involved coding, consumed more time than allocated, and it was imperative to make the vital parts and components working. As improvements, suggestions in upgrading the website can be: refining the model further on, loading and downloading from various devices such as handhelds, cellphones, or different GPS models. Actually, only one model has been tested, that is the garmin series, due to availability in local, but in the near future, other models may also be part of improvements. Another progressive tasks, will be precision in latitudes and longitunal information. Actually, google maps has a slight deflection in coordinates, and the author has notified google about it. Further to a gain of precision, coordinates will be updated, and can be made open to public usage.

PROJECT PRACTISE

Project development

Backpacking with GPS in Mauritius, was developed intentionally as a pilot system. So as to evaluate the fesibility of using GPS in the country, and what aid it could represent to inland users, as well as foreigners. As a matter of fact, the pilot approach build, was done satisfactorily, as planned. A real system, on the other hand, would take much more time, for instance, collecting data is one key factor to consider: all the fuelling places in Mauritius, or capture of the police stations and government institutions such as as banks, points of currency changes. Another aspect, could be to the expensiveness, as such a system would require considerable resources in terms of equipments and maintenance. As the pilot project is conclusive today, one can plan a proper system, and estimate the cost of resources easier.

Languages to development are open to the public, although it requires skills in programming. At this stage, the author has had to view tutorials, document himself, before developing. HTML at first sight was easiest, to preparing the interfaces, and gradually, the skills needed climbed higher, as it comes to ASP. Connecting databases, are the ultimate ways and most effective through asp constructs. Scripts, were placed, while interacting components altogether, to facilitate functionality between pages. For example, scripts were to connect, read and write onto databases and XML files. The scripting and connections were most challenging, as it was a first occurrence to the author for developing.

Challenges encountered

During the development phase, some challenges were met across, and steps to cross over, were as follows:

1. Deflection error on gps against google maps
   GPS readings were different to that of google maps.

   Measures taken: Although the garmin nuvi model showed precise information, it did not correspond to google maps. The latters' longitunal and latitudes were taken as samples, and records of garmin collected, for future updating. User has notified google of the problem, and hopefully , maps will soon be updated.

2. Hosting
   Local ISP supplier provides website hosting, but only for html pages.

Measures taken: a second free hosting place was found, www.somee.com. ASP pages worked fine, but when images are integrated in interface pages, it does not load. Finally, a third hosting place was tried, which appears to be excellent, and hosts combination of database, asp, php, vbscripting, and html as well as images. The site is http://aspspider.ws . Only issue is that the free period is for 90 days, subsequently sufficient for after-implementation.

SUMMARY

The evaluations chapter, is a walkthrough of objectives, finding out whether all the objective segments, in relation to each project part, is fulfilled or not. Further to, chapters appraisals through the methodologies used, against those of what has been proposed, has been compared. Almost all are aligned to the PID, and chapters of the report, although time slices may have been slightly overlapped during implementation. In addition to, constraints have been voiced, and also further considerations of improvements.

CHAPTER 8

CONCLUSIONS

At this point, where development and report writing is done, we now conclude on the overall project and its applications, as per to different levels, in the local community or abroad, socially, or even business-wise. Lastly, we will have a focus of what future developments, can bring to the system.

Areas of applications:

Firstly, lets see the different application areas, that can adopt such a project, for better advantages:

- ✓ Fire services: nearest water points, and stations.
- ✓ Emergency charts: that can prove to be useful to the public(police stations information, hospitals, dental cares etc)
- ✓ Blind people: equipped with voiced GPS, others can plan the routes, and load, while blind people can find their way better.

Overall benefits, are also to be considered:

- ➢ Better estimates of trips, resulting in decrease in cost of driving and refuelling.
- ➢ Better holiday planning
- ➢ Saves time: plan a route, and you don't loose yourself at any part of the country.
- ➢ Motivates people to travel around

As we can see, applications of the project, spans on a broad view; and people can use, benefit from them. In addition to, it can be applied to community work, and contribute to helping people in society.

PROJECT'S APPRAISAL

Much to the author's efforts, a lot was experienced and acquired. Self learning abilities were developed, at the intent of precision in analysis, design and development focus. Now I can better analyse, develop situations that I could not do previously. It also helps us, to refine our methods, understanding and applying new techniques better.In terms, it also enhances one's capacity to handle larger projects, in the future, being confident on what I can do, as a student.

THE FUTURE

In occurrence, GPS plotting, is now into our era. Once our maps reaches a good level of precision, it will be taken as a baseline, for automated vehicles. Automated piloting, is one way of perceiving the future development.

As the IEE report says, "Cybercars and dual mode vehicles are presently the most innovative testbeds for vehicular automation applications" GPS, and maps may contribute a lot to automatic guiding of vehicles in the near future

Extract:
http://ieeexplore.ieee.org/Xplore/login.jsp?url=http%3A%2F%2Fieeexplore.ieee.or g%2Fiel5%2F11180%2F36023%2F01707389.pdf&authDecision=-203

Surely, this is one way to perceive what is coming on, and once the precise baseline is built, more avenues will show up.

REFERENCE

Referencing is mostly from web resources, with a few books, along the way:

Books:

Roger S. Pressman, 1982. Software Enineering, a pratitioner's approach, fourth edition: McGRAW-HILL INTERNATIONAL EDITIONS.

Paul Bocij, Dave Chaffey, Andrew Greasley, 2003. Business information systems, technology, development and management for the e-business, second edition: Dave Chaffey.

Rory Burke, 2003. Project Management, Planning and Control Techniques: Wiley.

David King, Dennis Viehland, Jae Lee, 2006. Electronic Commerce, A Managerial Perspective: Efraim Turban.

Electronic General Sources

University of Portsmouth, 2007. Referencing@portsmouth. Retrived this 10th of July 2009, from:

http://referencing.port.ac.uk/apa/index.html

W3 schools, 1999-2009. Retrieved the 7th of June 2009, from the w3schools website:

http://www.w3schools.com/

Mauritius Meteorological Services(2005). Retrieved the 21st of June 2009,from

http://metservice.intnet.mu/

Google Maps API, 2009. Retrieved the 2nd of june 2009, from the google website:

http://code.google.com/apis/maps/

Web Wiz Guide, 2001-2009. Retrieved this 18th of June 2009, from:

http://www.webwizguide.com

Aspin, 1999-2009. Asp tutorials and code snips. Retrieved this 19th of June 2009, from http://www.aspin.com/home/tutorial

Electronic-Tourism

Mauritius Tourism Promotion Authority Official Website, Retrieved the 28th of December 2008, from http://www.tourism-mauritius.mu/

Mauritius Chamber of Commerce and Industries, Hotels and Restaurants Sector, Retrieved the 28th of December 2008, from http://www.mcci.org/E_tourism.htm

Ed Harris,ED(2008). Mauritius Tourism Sees Slower Growth in 2008, retrieved the 28th of December 2008, from http://uk.reuters.com/article/oilRpt/idUKL2661267520080626

Air Mauritius, retrieved the 28th of December 2008, from http://www.airmauritius.com/

World Travel and Tourism Council, retrieved the 28th of December 2008, from http://www.wttc.org/eng/Tourism_Research/Tourism_Satellite_Accounting/TSA_C ountry_Reports/Mauritius

Eric Ng Ping Cheun(ENPC). Global financial crisis hits Mauritius' stock and property management, retrieved this 28th of December 2008, from http://www.africanexecutive.com/modules/magazine/articles.php?article=3715

Philip English(PE) 2008, from the Economic Development Institute, The World Bank. Mauritius, reigniting the engines of growth, A teaching case study. Retrieved this 28th of December 2008, from http://siteresources.worldbank.org/WBI/Resources/wbi37136.pdf

Mauritius excursions, retrieved this 26th of January 2009, from

http://www.mauriclick.com/mauritius/excursions/activities.htm

Mauritius Tourism Promotion Authority Official Website. Retrieved the 22nd of February 2009, from http://www.tourism-mauritius.mu/

Grandbaie.mu, village touristique balneaire. Retrieved the 22nd of February 2009, from http://www.grandbaie.mu

The best tropical islands, Mauritius. Retrieved the 22nd of February 2009, from http://www.besttropicalislandsintheworld.com/mauritius/

Mauritius   travel.   Retrieved   the   22nd   of   February   2009,   from
http://www.travelmauritius.info

Discover Mauritius. Retrieved the 22nd of February 2009, from www.mauritius.net

Mauritius   Portal,   island   info.   Retrieved   the   22nd   of   February   2009,   from
http://www.islandinfo.mu

Xplore Mauritius. Retrieved from http://www.xploremauritius.com

Electronic-GPS navigations

Indianapolis. Retrieved this 10th of january 2009 from:

http://bp2.trimbleoutdoors.com/ViewTrip.aspx?tripId=255637

Trimble navigation limited, retrieved this 10th of January 2009 from

http://investor.trimble.com/releasedetail.cfm?ReleaseID=191008

Backpaker magazine, retrieved this 10th of January 2009 from

http://www.aimmedia.com/article_display_89.html

Backpacking GPS maps, retrieved this 10th of January 2009, from

http://www.accuterra.com/products/accuterra_layers/outdoor-trail-maps

GPS maps retrieved this 16th of January 2009 from

http://rwsmaps.griffel.se/

Travel by GPS retrieved this 16th of January 2009 from

http://www.travelbygps.com/

GPS coordinate converter, retrieved this 16th of January 2009, from

http://boulter.com/gps/

GPS maps of all kinds, retrieved this 16th of January 2009, from http://www.gps-practice-and-fun.com/gps-maps.html

Foreca weather, retrieved this 26th of January 2009, from

www.foreca.com

Electronic-programming

Google maps real time GPS tracker, retrieved this 17th of May 2009, from
http://conversationswithmyself.com/maps/tracker/gmapTracker.html

Interating google maps into your web applications, retrieved this 4th of May 2009,
from

http://www.developer.com/java/web/article.php/10935_3528381_2

Google code, Ajax API's playground. Retrieved this 4th of may 2009, from

http://code.google.com/apis/ajax/playground/?exp=maps#show_terrain

Microsoft help and support, July 1 2004. How to connect an html page into a
Microsoft access database. Retrieved this 4th of May 2009, from

http://support.microsoft.com/kb/308459

Electronic Sources-Miscellaneous

http://www.barelyfitz.com/projects/slideshow/index.php/4

PHP, retrieved this 10th april 2009, from:

http://www.php.net/manual/en/intro-whatis.php

Enhanced ER diagrams, retrieved this 18th april 2009, from:

http://www.cse.ohio-state.edu/~gurari/course/cse670/cse670Ch16.xht

EER diagrams, retrieved this 18th april 2009, from:

http://mail.gnome.org/archives/dia-list/2006-December/msg00026.html

Extended entity relationships, retrieved this 19th april 2009, from:

http://sdm.lbl.gov/OPM/DM_TOOLS/OPM/ER/node3.html

APPENDIX-COMPETITOR ANALYSIS

Website: www.tourism-mauritius.mu

Content: information about Mauritius, as an island. Discovering, experiencing Mauritius, and a trade corner.

Presentation: Mauritius is presented as a tourism product: An attractive island, with all necessary resources and modern facilities, to capture the eye of the holiday planners.

Aim : The site is owned by the Mauritius Tourism Promotion Authority. As its name states, its aim is to promote Mauritius as an island to foreign traders, and tourists.

Brief: Being the primary entity, responsible for tourism promotion in Mauritius, the MTPA, as its aim suggests, provides an overall view of Mauritius, through a blend of its best places, and attractions. Although the site has an excellent design, in promoting the island's image, it does not aim to attract backpakers, or provide instructive information of about travelling within the island. Hence, MTPA, promotes tourism, for first class travellers, with an expensive budgeting.

Website: www.grandbaie.mu

Content: information about a village in Mauritius that welcomes tourists at very high rates. News, lodging places, restaurants, shopping are all static information. No presence of maps/layouts, contact information though.

Presentation: Presentation of the village as a tourist station, with all amenities and facilities, but without proper contact information and addresses.

Aim: the site is primarily set, to attract incomers to this particular village, and also enhance leisure and lifestyle activities in that particular area.

Brief: The site promotes all aspects within a village in the north of the island: The activities, shopping places and attractions, as well as news boards. Despite a casual appearance, the site also captures shopping malls of first class tourism, as well as food and lodging perspectives. The lifestyle in grandbaie, here, is appealing. It is wise, to understand though, that different villages offer different splendours, and contribute to a share of the local culture in Mauritius. These aspects miss the abilities of the sightseer or traveller going to different parts of the island.

Website: www.mauritius.net

Content: fewer information about sight seeing, travelling: An operator's website, proposing trip packages and car rentals.

Presentation: the natural cachet is presented first, as an attractive island, and besides, the business aspect is revealed: booking online tickets, and preparing for holidays in Mauritius.

Aim: B2C website. Business to client, making profits is the aim.

Brief: The site, offers online bookings, and shows places of interest to a common market share. That is, a market share that the owner has interest in. Along with the aim, the site offers only certain aspects that owner intends to make profits, and grow his business activities. A perspective which is only part of the islands' natural places, and hooks the independent traveler, to the typical businessman's net.

Website: http://www.islandinfo.mu

Content: few records of places around Mauritius: shopping, activities, restaurants, nightlife. Promotes hotels & site is full of adverts.

Presentation: seems as a leisure portal, but with few places to see, and lots of places to spend money.

Aim: leisure portal, but with a lucrative aim.

Brief: Lively, with plenty of advertisements, the site demonstrates a glamorous Mauritian society. Although well structured, it has few records to please the independent traveler. A flavor of business shows the side intents of the website, with places to stay such as middle class hotels and tours. The information of how to travel, where to travel information is unfortunately not available, on this site.

Summary: Through the samples selected, as competitors, each has its own aims, and hence, the site adheres to such. Although some have excellent designs, it does not contribute much to help, or adhere to an independent travelers plan. Some that comes close to this aim, are either business aimed, showing only parts of what can be visited, or very few records, of the low-cost accessibilities of the island.

Introduction

Mauritius, a small country in the Indian ocean, is well known for its golden beaches and natural habitat. Surrounded by the sea, and coral reefs, the lagoons have always provided shallow waters, and fishing, as well as many activities, such as snorkelling, diving, water skiing and surfing. Through the centuries, the island has been reaping its main revenues from sugar cane cultivation and manufacturing. The economic aspect of the country was excellent, and our island flourished with the secured income of sugar cane. It was only recently, when the price of sugar cane came into decline, that the Mauritian government chose to favorise other sectors, to build up main economic pillars. One of them, was tourism.

The latter being already a small sector, suddenly became the concern of all Mauritians. Many hotels were already along the coast. Incentives from the government, came into influencing massive campaigns like marketing, advertising, to promoting a better era for tourism growth. Inland tourism, security, training, events made the tourism flourish even better. Now the industry is one of the leading economic spines of our paradise island.

Through the years, the national airline, joined in the game too. It aligned its strategies to the tourism growth. The new slogan: "Air Mauritius, your preferred leisure airline", spiced up the tourism growth strategy. Clearly Mauritius had grounds to be a first class destination. The hotels climbed up with quality training & products, offering up to the outmost exigencies of the tourism market, such as luxurious lodgings, gastronomies and inland comfy travels.

Tourism now is at its peak in Mauritius. It is generating revenues of 40 billion rupees (source: http://www.mcci.org/E_tourism.htm) to the Mauritian economy. The peak periods, shows the healthy driven sector, pushed by high class clients, from around the world. Despite the enormous revenues, and such reapings, vulnerable points and threats, are perpetually mountain hiking, the developed sector. One of the weakest points of a high class tourism industry, is the dependency on the pull of its clients. Such aspect, if low in occurence, can be a threat to the huge operating costs, and hence, crumble down the hotels and services.

As a matter of fact, the fears came into reality. The ending year of 2008, shows that global recession impacts, will definitely crop into the tourism sector. Hotels, are now at a booking rate of around 30 to 50 per cent, which is half, compared   to   the   usual   end   of   year   bookings. (http://uk.reuters.com/article/oilRpt/idUKL2661267520080626). Climbing into the train, is the effects of recession, although Mauritius has an excellent environment, for nurturing tourism.

In view to consolidate the incoming rate of clients, it is envisaged to build an atmosphere of middle class tourism. Hikers, sightseers and backpakers could as well contribute to the economic spine. People mixing, in the ordinary lives of Mauritius, could be another flavour of tourism market in Mauritius.

Insight of project

This project, is aimed to provide, information directly to middle class tourists, through a web content delivery, so they can travel their own, visiting the island, at their ease. Through such contents, foreigners can travel inland, knowing the country's places of visits and useful information, such as fuelling, lodging and trips. A website, with all the features and information of the island's geography, places of visits and services, will be the effective tool, to communicate & promote information with those who wishes to mingle into the daily Mauritian life.

One of the main aspects is to publish, via web, the exact coordinates, and route plans of sightseeing trips. Hence, someone can use the web site, with a measuring device, like a GPS, to drive precisely around the island, and obtain needy information, on travelling.

In addition to, fuelling places, lodging and restaurants will be pointed onto a local map, which are the essential parts of a travel. Other key aspects will involve adverts of services, of places of interests, bungalow owners, and small hotels, as well as transports facilitators(contract cars, vans, taxis)

Aim

Aim is to make use of suitable technologies, to create a website with mapping layers of the country's routes, places of interest, and corresponding geometry. The web layout will be an instructive material, to backpackers and travelers and even inland sight seers.

Objectives in meeting the aim

The objectives to be met are numerous. First is to find suitable maps, and digitizing them in a suitable format, and hence, layering proceeds. To feed the maps with information, data collection needs to be done and Google Earth, will be an aid to such development, and well as a GPS device, to record precise geometric places. These primary steps, together with the detailed objectives are further defined below:

1. *Reading, research and documentation of existing products, competitors etc..*

2. *Analysis*
    a. Define needs(google earth, mapping software, GPS)
    b. Gather information about the needs (software, hardware, programming language, skills)
    c. Evaluate cost and availability of needs
    d. Selection of needs
    e. Gather information about places of interests and capture coordinates, route information etc.
    f. Gather information of available services(fuelling, lodging etc)

3. *Design*
    a. Create design interface model
    b. Create a first layout of geographic island
    c. Add onto layers of information sets(fuel places, lodgings, etc)
    d. Provide a storage structure(maps, layers, information and pictures, as samples)
    e. Web layout((a)-(d))
    f. Print formats and layouts, exports(To GPS devices)
    g. Refine and revise model

4. *Implementation*
    a. Creation of website(registrations, interface etc)
    b. Upload basic maps, and layouts, with information store
    c. Refine & revise to working model
    d. Upload full features, and mappings, with information

5. *Testing & final*
    a. Test runs

    b. Sample data feeding and tests
    c. Maintenance plans
    d. Backup, and security measures
    e. End note.

Applications proposal

The project, will be a blend, of geographical representations and web formats. Such development will be done, with the necessary programming tools and various web-based applications, in view to create easy to use webpages. Tools such as google earth, freely available GIS, and "map exporting/importing" applications, will be downloaded from the web itself, in view to provide a suitable method for development. A telecommunications company, will also be contacted, in view, to envisage GPS exportations(experimental), onto cellphones, equipped with GPS.

The analysis and design phase, steps of project reviews, design walkthroughs will be elaborated, in order to produce an improving web site. Moreover, usual updates and upgrades will be considered along, as often new programming tools help to render better designs.

Requirements

The functional requirements

1. Store maps, pictures, textual information
2. Store coordinates, organisations details
3. Store of services & miscellaneous information
4. Allow browsing/searching/exports/imports and printouts
5. Securing displayed information (backups, restrictions. . .)
6. Misc

The non-functional & performance requirements

1. Provide security of information
2. Allow a large quantity of users as well as quick multiprocessing facilities
3. Reports of hits, and user browsing
4. Capacity to store large volumes of pictures, maps and text information
5. Secured level access, to modify information displayed.

Technical requirements

1. Server, with fast processing capabilities, or similar hardware
2. GPS tracker(hand held device)
3. Operating system

4. Webserver
5. Applications(google earth, freely available tools like GIS, etc)
6. Hardware maintenance
7. Secondary server

Usability

1. Provide display to conventional 15" and 17"
2. Standard fonts, 9-12 characters, with thumbnail and high resolution pictures

Ethical Overview

As Mauritius is a multicultural society, the system will promote mix of cultures, as well as peaceful life of citizens: a special page, with pictures will show our cultural blend, in different festivities. Hence, the ethics, will be of naturally neutral and binding, as scope, and show our stability as an emerging developed country.

System architecture

The system will consist essentially of a website, onto a server, with a fast internet connection, as start. Upon growth of, system will hence be enveloped with security, and better hardware, networking and software, as well as administrative staff. The information will be stored in a database, and backed up regularly.

Project deliverables

A GPS recorder will be used to find the routes, to places of interest, and a digital camera, to show pictures of the islands most beautiful places. Further to, these, will be annexed with textual information and geographical information, via a web display. Pictures, such as the first place where people settled, the first harbour and forts, historic places of the country, will stand as artefacts, of our paradise island.

Project constraints

Time factor is one of the most prominent constraint. Acquaintance, meeting bungalow owners, restaurant owners and other service owners will be a major task, so as to obtain valid information, like routings. Time has to be found, to travel to the corners of the island and photo shots taken, as gps recordings as well. These will be done along, the months of data capture.

Resources such as hardware, needs also to be found, as a first instance. Since the project will not be a lucrative one at kick-off, some basic funding will be needed to launch the website and buy accompanying hardware, such as GPS recorders.

Skills, needs to be within the project development. As I am in networking, I will need to master the website development concepts and internet web designing, as well as GIS experience, to venture on.

Project approach

The project, will be made through the basic phases of development, that is requirements gathering, analysis, design, development and testing/maintenance. The analysis and design phases, will be closely linked, as analysing and refining information will render a better design. For data gathering, I will collect on my own, using my car, I have a digital camera and some contacts within the tourism industry.

Research will be done, before design phases, that is web references, books on how to build a good website and digitise the geographic maps, and apply a binding database onto. Finally contacting souvenir shops will be the endnote to development, as they can advertise their products on web.

Facilities & resources

The facilities I have actually, is a car, a digital camera, and web resources. Moreover, Mauritius is a small island, so I can contact owners very easily.

As I have my own personal computer at home, with a permanent 128k adsl line connected to interne. This will be a first platform to run the website/and backup. External disks, which I also have, will be used as secondary backup media. Internet will be my research place, and well as ebooks, on how to create & develop websites. Moreover, A regular, daily, time slot will be allocated to the project research, 2 hours, for instance, so as to keep up with the documentations, readings and research.

Log of risks

The first risk encountered will be finding the right mix of hardware and software for development phase. Much experience is needed, and if the time allocated to research and documentation, is not observed due to prior works(professional or family), then the level of expertise may be affected.

Second risk, is the availability of contacts & resources, as well as the time to record routes. Routes will have to be recorded and planned, and as it is time consuming, I will have to set myself to task during the weekends. Time could be a cropping constraints if there happens to be rainy, and acts of god happenings during weekends. In view to propose services, we will need to contact people, offering tourism entertainment and to acquaint and propose our own services to the tourist service suppliers, we need a firm ground, and a university project is sometimes, a weak proposal intent, as business.

Third, is to find proper hardware. GPS recorders are costly, and they are rare in Mauritius. The proper GPS device needs to be found, and purchased over internet(which could take some time to come to Mauritius). Another factor to be considered is definitely, the GPS signal captures. Hopefully, almost all parts of the island have satellite coverage, so I can do recordings.

Starting point for research

The internet will be my primary resource, for research. In turn, gathering information across the island, on site pictures, will be my second source of income for research within Mauritius.

Along I will try to get in touch with people already working with handheld gps devices, so i can have an idea with the designs and implementations phase.

Breakdown of tasks

1. *Reading, research and documentation of existing products, competitors . . .*
    a. Competitors list, and information availability
    b. List of products available to order
    c. List of resources and how to access them
    d. Miscellaneous reading
2. *Analysis*
    a. Define needs
        i. Hardware

      ii. Software

     iii. Skills

     iv. Financing and others

b. Gather information about the needs (software, hardware, programming language, skills)

      i. Hardware: evaluation of what the project needs, prices & availability

      ii. Software: Evaluation of what the project needs, availability, accessibility and portability

     iii. Skills: What is needed to practice, and refining

     iv. Miscellaneous(financing needs, physical spaces, security needs)

c. Evaluate cost and availability of needs

      i. Costing for each item mentioned above

      ii. Total Cost expected, and where to obtain

d. Selection of needs

      i. List of software & hardware selected

      ii. Time available

     iii. Misc

e. Gather information about places of interests and capture coordinates, route information etc.

      i. Factors affecting the tasks(weather & other constraints

      ii. Planning of trips

         1. Capture trip information

         2. Storage and treatment of captured information

     iii. Others

f. Gather information about available services

      i. List of various small hotel lodgings and how to contact them

      ii. List of all fuel companies, and how to obtain information about their outlets

     iii. List of eco tourism services(parks, nature reserves, quad, biking)

     iv. List of bungalow owners & taxi services

     v. Misc

3. *Design*

a. Create design interface model

      i. Use, from collected, data that can be prone to provide good webpages

      ii. Create templates & structure of web(pages, links etc)

     iii. Build first model with basic information(pictures, and plain information

b. Create a first layout of geographical island

      i. Use existing templates, available scans, to produce layouts of the island's geography.

      ii. Add-ons

     iii. Practice to better layout model

     iv. Misc

c. Add onto layers of information(fuel places, lodgings etc)

      i. Method to add layers

      ii. Templates, and information adding to layers

iii. Misc

    d. Provide a storage structure(maps, information and pictures, as samples)
        i. Creating a storage structure plan for the different information
        ii. Linking the storage plan, to different maps ,and layouts
    e. Print formats and layouts, exports(to GPS devices)
        i. Ensure good printing formats, for routes, informations etc
        ii. Add-up browsing modes and miscellaneous option
        iii. Experimental- defining method for exporting GPS info to cellphones, or mobile devices
        iv. Trial of method
    f. Refine and revise model
        i. Review & revise creation model
        ii. Review & revise storage structure
        iii. Review & revise imports, export and mappings
        iv. Misc

4. *Implementation*
    a. Creation of website
        i. Register domain names, and upload on web
        ii. Misc
    b. Upload basic maps and layouts, with information store
        i. Assembly of a working model online
        ii. Validations & refining
        iii. Refine and revise
    c. Refine and revise to working model
        i. Walkthough
        ii. Misc
    d. Upload full features and mappings, with information store
        i. Maps, linked with information store
        ii. Misc
        iii. Ensure working model for all options
        iv. Security
        v. Misc

5. *Testing & final*
    a. Test runs
        i. Administrator's input, and modifications of information
    b. Sample data feeding and tests
        i. Boundary value analysis & other testing methods devised
        ii. Misc
    c. Maintenance plans
        i. Brief on how to maintain the project(costs incurred)
        ii. User Manual
    d. Backup and security measures
        i. Backup measures to be taken-backup plan
        ii. Security measures- Hardware & software
    e. End note.

i. Conclusion

Project plan

Annexed is the Gantt chart, which shows the tasks line(sub tasks minimised), of the project's lifetime:

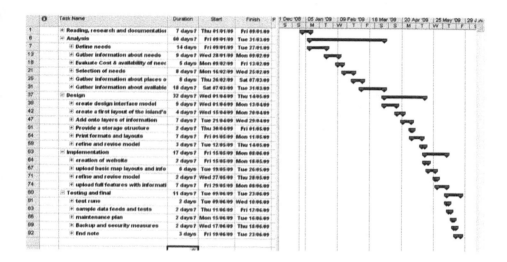

Network Diagram

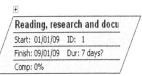

⊞

Reading, research and docu

Start: 01/01/09	ID: 1
Finish: 09/01/09	Dur: 7 days?
Comp: 0%	

⊞

Analysis

Start: 09/01/09	ID: 6
Finish: 31/03/09	Dur: 60 days?
Comp: 0%	

⊞

Design

Start: 01/04/09	ID: 37
Finish: 14/05/09	Dur: 32 days?
Comp: 0%	

⊞

Implementation

Start: 15/05/09	ID: 63
Finish: 08/06/09	Dur: 17 days?
Comp: 0%	

⊞

Testing and final

Start: 09/06/09	ID: 80
Finish: 23/06/09	Dur: 11 days?
Comp: 0%	

Legal, Ethical, Professional and Social Issues

Information uploaded, and used throughout the project, will be trusted copyright, as pictures, and photo loads needs to represent the true conditions of the country in view to appeal foreigners to come to Mauritius. Information will be given a professional treat, asking service suppliers, which types of info they need to display, and how would they like so.

An aspect of the website, will be publishing photos of real life, of people living in Mauritius, that is the social ties, the religious ceremonies and the harmonious cultural blend. An aspect that adheres entirely to promoting peaceful staying environments.

A picture is worth a thousand words, a Chinese proverb once said. Thereon, may it be a unique experience of coming to visit a paradise island.

APPENDIX 2-INTERVIEW TRANSCRIPTS

Interview transcripts: as a matter of convenience, most interviews have been transcripted, from my own words, with an overall idea of what the user wants to voice out. Moreover, it is quite impossible to list all the records collected, so, some important ones have been annexed here, basically each from a different business type.

Owner 1:

Business type: restaurant

After preliminary introductions and briefs

Question: what are your marketing tools?

Answer: Normally people walk across and see my board sign, or activities.

From ear to mouth

Occasional posting on magazines

Question: Do you use the internet?

Answer: It is not in my everyday life, but I understand the concepts, usage of it, as a tool.

Question: How would you describe internet, as a marketing tool?

Answer: Some people use it as an advertising tool, and I have some friends with the same businesses, using the internet. But I'm not sure of what it can reap.

Question: What if, you had a place to advertise, low cost, showing your exact location within Mauritius, and means to contact you?

Answer: the concept of internet is growing from day to day, and I would say it is an interesting offer; still the conditions, need to be known..

Owner 2:

Business type: restaurant

After preliminary introductions and briefs

Question: what are your marketing tools?

Answer: cards, magazines, email.

From ear to mouth

Question: Do you use the internet?

Answer: yes, to check emails and new recipes. I receive regular updates of recipes online.

Question: How would you describe internet, as a marketing tool?

Answer: It can be..

Question: What if, you had a place to advertise, low cost, showing your exact location within Mauritius, and means to contact you?

Answer: Seems interesting, if it reaps more than my previous advertisement means.

Owner 3:

Business type: Big hotel

After preliminary introductions and briefs

Question: how do you market hotel rooms?

Answer: tour operators, travel agencies

Question: and how is the internet coupled into your enterprise?

Answer: I offer it as a service to tourists, we have a website for our hotel.

Question: in a few words, the website does?

Answer: Promoting our name, reputation. More, it offers information about rooms.

Question: would you like to be listed in a popular website, with exact driving locations, and direct contact information?

Answer: its all welcomed, as I spend lots in advertising. I spend every mean to get clients in.

Owner 4:

Business type: small/medium hotel

After preliminary introductions and briefs

Question: how do you market hotel rooms?

Answer: tour operators, travel agencies, adverts

Question: and how is the internet coupled into your enterprise?

Answer: we have email as contacting means, and a main hall that offers internet access.

Question: Do you receive lots of requests through mail?

Answer: mostly the operators communicate to us, for booking and so; but direct mail from clients seldoms arrives.

Question: would you like to annexed your email & communications, onto a website, that offers direction locations of your business, along with other listings?

Answer: if not too expensive, I would appreciate a trial basis, and see how it goes..

Owner 5:

Business type: transport(taxi service)

After preliminary introductions and briefs

Question: how do you find clients?

Answer: on stand-by at airports or hotel parkings.

Question: do u use internet/email?

Answer: rarely.

Question: how would you find email/internet, if accessible, as an aid to your business?

Answer: I am on the move everyday. Unless I have a mobile device to check, or use, I find it inappropriate, as to communicate to clients.

Question: what if your services were exposed on a website, on internet, with your contact information?

Answer: maybe that perspective could be interesting, depending on the price..

APPENDIX 3-INTERVIEW TRANSCRIPTS

Record collections

Records basically possess the same fields, but the type differs. Restaurants, hotels, or hospitals all have latitudes and longitudes that have been plotted out. As the plot samples have been numerous, 10 or 20 for each type, I will post 5 of each here, so as to have an idea of how implementation can be.

Business name: Chez Patrick

Address: Royal Road, Mahebourg

Latitude: -20.411891

Longitude: 57.706032

Type: restaurant

Business name: Le gris gris

Address: Souillac

Latitude: -20.51868

Longitude: 57.528534

Type: restaurant

Business name: Choice food palace

Address: Route St Paul, Phoenix

Latitude: -20.287317

Longitude: 57.50776

Type: restaurant

Business name: Red lobster

Address: Comlone branch road, nouvelle france

Latitude: -20.374038

Longitude: 57.562866

Type: restaurant

Business name: Debonnairs pizza

Address: Port Louis

Latitude: -20.163288

Longitude: 57.503901

Type: restaurant

Business name: Hotel amber

Address: east coast

Latitude: -20.190357

Longitude: 57.774868

Type: hotel

Business name: Hotel casuarina

Address: in the north

Latitude: -20.039483

Longitude: 57.542953

Type: hotel

Business name: Club mediterranee

Address: Royal road, pointe aux cannoniers

Latitude: -19.989643

Longitude: 57.590675

Type: hotel

Business name: Le prince Maurice

Address: East coast

Latitude: -20.1633449

Longitude: 57.745686

Type: hotel

Business name: Hotel casuarina

Address: in the north

Latitude: -20.039483

Longitude: 57.542953

Type: hotel

Business name: Hilton

Address: East coast

Latitude: -20.29259

Longitude: 57.363095

Type: hotel

Business name: Le tropical

Address: East coast

Latitude: -20.253984

Longitude: 57.797871

Type: hotel

Photo

Reference:

Latitude:

Longitude:

Route layout

Reference: 001

Latitude 1: -20.17456745

Longitude 1: 57.47497559

Latitude 2: -20.24931350

Longitude 2: 57.48321533

Latitude 3: -20.29053732

Longitude 3: 57.51342773

Latitude 4: - 20.38131984

Longitude 4: 57.57453918

Latitude 5: -20.42379544

Longitude 5: 57.65281677

Latitude 6: -20.41156882

Longitude 6: 57.70500183

Notes: Motorway from Port Louis, the city, to the airport, in the south.

APPENDIX 4 TEST CASES

TEST CASES

st segment	Ref	Test module	Input range	Objective	Expected results	Test priority
ack box	B1	Main interface load	web address	load main page on internet	Loads within secs	High
	B2	Click for sub pages	clicks	links to maps, gps, information and forum	Browse different pages	High
	B3	Maps page	clicks	Toggle options-hotels	Hide/view	Medium
	B4	Maps page	clicks	Toggle options-restaurants	Hide/view	Medium
	B5	Maps page	clicks	Toggle options-sight seeing	Hide/view	Medium
	B6	Maps page	clicks	Toggle options-Fuel places	Hide/view	Medium
	B7	Maps page	clicks	spots information	Show label to each spot	Medium
	B8	GPS page	clicks	Load GPX file	Browse/upload	Medium
	B9	GPS page	clicks	View initial location from GPS	View on map	Medium
	B10	GPS page	clicks	Draw series of lines	View polyline on browser	Medium
	B11	GPS page	clicks	Clear route	Clear polyline sets	Medium
	B12	GPS page	clicks	View GPS landmarks on text	View on screen	Medium
	B13	GPS page	clicks	View GPS landmarks on XML	View on screen	Medium
	B14	GPS page	clicks	Download points	View location on GPS	Medium
	B15	Information-add	0-9; 8 chrs	ID input	Should display only numbers	Medium
	B16	Information-add	a-z; 30 chrs	Name	Should display only letters, 30 max	Medium
	B17	Information-add	a-z; 0-9 50 chrs	Address	Display alphanumeric	Medium
	B18	Information-add	0-9; 12 chrs	Latitude	Display num, 8 digits, with decimal	Medium
	B19	Information-add	0-9; 12 chrs	Longitude	Display num, 8 digits, with decimal	Medium
	B20	Information-add	Selection	Choose type:hotel/restaurant/fuel	Display choice; user selects	Medium

	B21	Information-add	Selection	Choose region	Display choice; user selects	Medium
	B22	information-delete	0-9; 8 chrs	ID input	Should display only numbers	Medium
	B23	information-delete	a-z; 30 chrs	Name	Should display only letters, 30 max	Medium
	B24	information-delete	a-z; 0-9 50 chrs	Address	Display alphanumeric	Medium
	B25	information-delete	0-9; 12 chrs	Latitude	Display num, 8 digits, with decimal	Medium
	B26	information-delete	0-9; 12 chrs	Longitude	Display num, 8 digits, with decimal	Medium
	B27	information-delete	Selection	Choose type:hotel/restaurant/fuel	Display choice; user selects	Medium
	B28	information-delete	Selection	Choose region	Display choice; user selects	Medium
	B29	information-login	0-9; a-z	input user name & password	display if wronged	High
	B30	Gallery	clicks	Browse images	preview/back/forward moves	Medium
	B31	Forum-view	clicks	Browse previous notes	Display previous logs	Medium
	B32	Forum-add new	0-9; a-z	input new notes	Display after recorded	Medium
White box	W1	Database	add record	check if exists in database	Record available	High
	W2	Database	delete record	check if exists in database	Record not available	High
	W3	Database	add record	check if displayed on map	Record available	High
	W4	Database	delete record	check if displayed on map	Record not available	High
	W5	GPS	load	check if displayed on map	Point displayed	High
	W6	GPS	Download	check if displayed on GPS	Route displayed	Medium
	W7	Database	login	check if right user/password accessing	Should verify in database	High
Integrity	I 1	Surfing	clicks	check if all pages can be accessed	Should display all sub pages	High
	I2	Database	input	check if added record are displayed	Should display record	High
		Database	Clicks	Checks if deled records are displayed	Should not display record	High

TEST RESULTS

st segment	Ref	Test module	Input range	Expected results	Actual results	Status
ack box	B1	Main interface load	web address	Loads within secs	As expected	Success
	B2	Click for sub pages	clicks	Browse different pages	As expected	Success
	B3	Maps page	clicks	Hide/view	option is hidden/viewed on toggle	Success
	B4	Maps page	clicks	Hide/view	option is hidden/viewed on toggle	Success
	B5	Maps page	clicks	Hide/view	option is hidden/viewed on toggle	Success
	B6	Maps page	clicks	Hide/view	option is hidden/viewed on toggle	Success
	B7	Maps page	clicks	Show label to each spot	Label information shown	Success
	B8	GPS page	clicks	Browse/upload	file uploaded	Success
	B9	GPS page	clicks	View on map	Spot on map	Success
	B10	GPS page	clicks	View polyline on browser	Polylines in view appear	Success
	B11	GPS page	clicks	Clear polyline sets	As expected	Success
	B12	GPS page	clicks	View on screen	As expected	Success
	B13	GPS page	clicks	View on screen	As expected	Success
	B14	GPS page	clicks	View location on GPS	file saved into txt, must be converted into GPX	Halfway
	B15	Information-add	0-9; 8 chrs	Should display only numbers	As expected	Success
	B16	Information-add	a-z; 30 chrs	Should display only letters, 30 max	As expected	Success
	B17	Information-add	a-z; 0-9 50 chrs	Display alphanumeric	As expected	Success
	B18	Information-add	0-9; 12 chrs	Display num, 8 digits, with decimal	As expected	Success
	B19	Information-add	0-9; 12 chrs	Display num, 8 digits, with decimal	As expected	Success
	B20	Information-add	Selection	Display choice; user selects	As expected	Success
	B21	Information-add	Selection	Display choice; user selects	As expected	Success
	B22	information-delete	0-9; 8 chrs	Should display only numbers	As expected	Success

	B23	information-delete	a-z; 30 chrs	Should display only letters, 30 max	As expected	Success
	B24	information-delete	a-z; 0-9 50 chrs	Display alphanumeric	As expected	Success
	B25	information-delete	0-9; 12 chrs	Display num, 8 digits, with decimal	As expected	Success
	B26	information-delete	0-9; 12 chrs	Display num, 8 digits, with decimal	As expected	Success
	B27	information-delete	Selection	Display choice; user selects	As expected	Success
	B28	information-delete	Selection	Display choice; user selects	As expected	Success
	B29	information-login	0-9; a-z	display if wronged	prompts user to re-enter	Success
	B30	Gallery	clicks	preview/back/forward moves	slides show; back and forward works	Success
	B31	Forum-view	clicks	Display previous logs	views loaded	Success
	B32	Forum-add new	0-9; a-z	Display after recorded	views loaded	Success
White box	W1	Database	add record	Record available	Record found in database	Success
	W2	Database	delete record	Record not available	Record not found in database	Success
	W3	Database	add record	Record available	Record found in database	Success
	W4	Database	delete record	Record not available	Record not found in database	Success
	W5	GPS	load	Point displayed	Point loaded on screen	Success
	W6	GPS	Download	Route displayed		Halfway
	W7	Database	login	Should verify in database	login is checked in	Success
Integrity	I 1	Surfing	clicks	Should display all sub pages	As expected	Success
	I2	Database	input	Should display record	As expected	Success
		Database	Clicks	Should not display record	As expected	Success
Test segment	Ref	Test module	Aim	Expected results	Actual results	Status
Integrity	I10	delete	Ask user to delete	form load & input	input works	Success
	I11	deleteprocess	deleting records	looks for record & delete	as expected	Success

I12	enterdata	New record input	form load & input	input works	Success
I13	enterforum	New record input	form load & input	input works	Success
I14	forumprocess	Saves forum record	saves into database	works	Success
I15	gpsloadmodule	Load GPS points	load point on screen		Halfway
I16	login	request user input	form load & input	works fine	Success
I17	login	validates	check in db, and validates	as expected	Success
I18	mapstoggle	view spots	load coordinates from markerdata files	as expected	Success
I19	markerdata	exports from db	records in xml ,separated wit commas and roots	as expected	Success
I20	myalbum	loads pictures	loads album of pictures to browse	as expected	Success
I21	recordsetforum	view forum	loads record from forum table	as expected	Success
I22	routes	plot polylines	shows points in xml , distance	as expected	Success
I23	routes	loads GPS points	loads routes from GPS	loads file, reads, but no display	Halfway
I26	updatedata	request user input to update	form load & input	as expected	Success
I27	updateprocess	processing of updation	updates database		Halfway
I28	updatesave	saves record	update and save in db	as expected	Success
I29	viewprocess	loads each record	view on display in tabular format	as expected	Success
I30	viewprocessadmin	loads record and request other options	view more options than browsing	as expected	Success
I31	accesstoxml	pumps from db to xml	xml file of records	as expected	Success

APPENDIX 5 PLAGIARISM REPORT

TURNITIN ORIGINALITY REPORT

Matching Text displayed, full report available at (and on cd)
http://aspspider.ws/universityproject/Turnitin_Originality_Report_91978002.html

TURNITIN ORIGINALITY REPORT

final report by Yasir Nabee

From UoP Project Oct08 (UoP Project Oct08)

Processed on 07-13-09 4:06 AM PDTID: 91978002Word Count: 21678

Overall Similarity Index: 4%

APPENDIX 6-CODING

ACCESSTOXML

```
<%


'=== declare variables
Dim objConn, strConnect, strSQL, rs, tb, mdbFile, objFSO, xmlFile, objWrite


'=== filename variables
xmlFile = Server.MapPath("markerdata.xml")
mdbFile = Server.MapPath("gpsdatabase.mdb")


'=== tab character for xml file
tb = chr(9)


'=== instantiate objects
set objFSO  = Server.CreateObject( "Scripting.FileSystemObject" )
Set objConn = Server.CreateObject( "ADODB.Connection" )


'=== connect to database
objConn.Open "Provider=Microsoft.Jet.OLEDB.4.0;Data Source=" & mdbFile


'=== open/create xml file
If Not objFSO.FileExists( xmlFile ) Then objFSO.CreateTextFile( xmlFile )
set objWrite = objFSO.OpenTextFile( xmlFile, 2 )
```

```
'=== open the xml file
objWrite.WriteLine("<?xml version=""1.0"" encoding=""ISO-8859-1""?>")
objWrite.WriteLine("<marker>")


strSQL = "SELECT * FROM records"
Set rs = objConn.Execute(StrSQL)


'=== loop through results
Do While not rs.EOF
  objWrite.Write(tb & tb & "<marker name='" & rs("name") & "'" )
  objWrite.Write(tb & tb & " <address>" & rs("address") & "</address>")
  objWrite.Write(tb & tb & " <tel>" & rs("tel") & "</tel>")
  objWrite.Write(tb & tb & " <lat>" & rs("lat") & "</lat>")
  objWrite.Write(tb & tb & " <lng>" & rs("lng") & "</lng>")
  objWrite.Write(tb & tb & " <type>" & rs("type") & "</type>")
  objWrite.Write(tb & tb & " <region>" & rs("region") & "</region>")
  objWrite.WriteLine("")
   rs.MoveNext
Loop


'=== finish xml file
objWrite.WriteLine("</marker>")
objWrite.Close()


%>
```

ADMIN

<HTML>

<HEAD>

<TITLE>Admin database page</TITLE>

</HEAD>

<BODY>

{

background:url(morne12.jpg) no-repeat;

}

<HR>

Welcome administrator. here, we can update the database, which loads points on google maps.

<P><B><font color="white">To browse database: </P></B>

<INPUT type='button' name='Button1' value='View records!' onclick="window.location='http://aspspider.ws/universityproject/viewprocessadmin.asp'">

<P><B><font color="white">To delete records: </P></B>

```
<INPUT type='button' name='Button1' value='Delete records!'
onclick="window.location='http://aspspider.ws/universityproject/delete.asp'">


<P><B><font color="white">To add a new point:</P></B>

<INPUT type='button' name='Button1' value='Add records!'
onclick="window.location='http://aspspider.ws/universityproject/enterdata.asp'">


<P><B><font color="white">To update records: </P></B>

<INPUT type='button' name='Button1' value='Update records!'
onclick="window.location='http://aspspider.ws/universityproject/update.asp'">


<PRE>




<b><font color="black">Table of contents: </b> <b><a
href="mapstoggle.html"><font color="red">MAPS</a> </b> <b><a
href="routes.asp"><font color="red">GPS & ROUTES</a></b> <b><font
color="white"><a href="viewprocess.asp"><font
color="red">INFORMATION</a></b> <b><font color="white"><a
href="enterforum.asp"><font color="red">FORUM & FAQS </a></b> <b><font
color="white"><a href="login.html"><font color="red">DATABASE
ADMINISTRATION </a></b> <b><font color="white"><a
href="contact.html"><font color="red">CONTACT US </a></b> <b><font
color="white"><a href="uopproject.html"><font color="red">RETURN TO MAIN
PAGE </a></b> </PRE>

<PRE>

</P>

<HR>
```

```
</BODY>


</HTML>
```

CLSUPLOAD

```
<%
' -------------------------------------------------------------------------------
' Container of Field Properties
Class clsField
        Public FileName
        Public ContentType
        Public Value
        Public FieldName
        Public Length
        Public BinaryData
End Class
' -------------------------------------------------------------------------------
Class clsUpload
' -------------------------------------------------------------------------------
        Private nFieldCount
        Private oFields()
        Private psFileFullPath
        Private psError
        Private psFileInputName
' -------------------------------------------------------------------------------
        Public Property Get Count()
                Count = nFieldCount
```

```
        End Property

' ------------------------------------------------------------------------

        Public Default Property Get Field(ByRef asFieldName)
                Dim lnLength
                Dim lnIndex


                lnLength = UBound(oFields)


                If IsNumeric(asFieldName) Then
                        If lnLength >= asFieldName And asFieldName > -1 Then
                                Set Field = oFields(asFieldName)
                        Else
                                Set Field = New clsField
                        End If
                Else
                        For lnIndex = 0 To lnLength
                                If LCase(oFields(lnIndex).FieldName) =
LCase(asFieldName) Then
                                        Set Field = oFields(lnIndex)
                                        Exit Property
                                End If
                        Next
                        Set Field = New clsField
                End If
        End Property

' ------------------------------------------------------------------------
```

```vb
Public Function Exists(ByRef avKeyIndex)

    Exists = Not IndexOf(avKeyIndex) = -1

End Function
```

'--

```vb
Public Property Get ValueOf(ByRef avKeyIndex)

    Dim lnIndex

    lnIndex = IndexOf(avKeyIndex)

    if lnIndex = -1 Then Exit Property

    ValueOf = oFields(lnIndex).Value

End Property
```

'--

```vb
Public Property Get FileNameOf(ByRef avKeyIndex)

    Dim lnIndex

    lnIndex = IndexOf(avKeyIndex)

    if lnIndex = -1 Then Exit Property

    FileNameOf = oFields(lnIndex).FileName

End Property
```

'--

```vb
Public Property Get LengthOf(ByRef avKeyIndex)

    Dim lnIndex

    lnIndex = IndexOf(avKeyIndex)

    if lnIndex = -1 Then Exit Property

    LengthOf = oFields(lnIndex).Length

End Property
```

'--

```vb
Public Property Get BinaryDataOf(ByRef avKeyIndex)
```

```
        Dim lnIndex

        lnIndex = IndexOf(avKeyIndex)

        if lnIndex = -1 Then Exit Property

        BinaryDataOf = oFields(lnIndex).BinaryData

    End Property
' -------------------------------------------------------------------------------

    Private Function IndexOf(ByVal avKeyIndex)

        Dim lnIndex


        If avKeyIndex = "" Then

            IndexOf = -1

        ElseIf IsNumeric(avKeyIndex) Then

            avKeyIndex = CLng(avKeyIndex)

            If nFieldCount > avKeyIndex And avKeyIndex > -1 Then

                IndexOf = avKeyIndex

            Else

                IndexOf = -1

            End If

        Else

            For lnIndex = 0 To nFieldCount - 1

                If LCase(oFields(lnIndex).FieldName) =
LCase(avKeyIndex) Then

                    IndexOf = lnIndex

                    Exit Function

                End If

            Next
```

```
                    IndexOf = -1

               End If

          End Function
' ----------------------------------------------------------------------------

Public Property Let FileFullPath(sValue)

     psFileFullPath = sValue

End Property

'
  _____
  _____

Public Property Get FileFullPath()

     FileFullPath = psFileFullPath

End Property
' ----------------------------------------------------------------------------

Public Property Let FileInputName(sValue)

     psFileInputName = sValue

End Property
' --------------------        ----------------------------------------------------

Public Function Save()

     if psFileFullPath <> "" and psFileInputName <> "" then

               'Save to connectionless client side recordset, write to stream,

               'and persist stream.


               'would think you should be able to write directly to

               'stream without recordset, but I could not get that to work


               On error resume next
```

```
binData = o.BinaryDataOf(psFileInputName)


set rs = server.createobject("ADODB.RECORDSET")

rs.fields.append "FileName", 205, LenB(binData)

rs.open

rs.addnew

rs.fields(0).AppendChunk binData


if err.number = 0 then

        set objStream = Server.CreateObject("ADODB.Stream")

        objStream.Type  = 1

        objStream.Open

        objStream.Write rs.fields("FileName").value

        objStream.SaveToFile psFileFullPath, 2

        objStream.close

        set objStream = Nothing


ENd if

rs.close

set rs = nothing

psError = Err.Description
else

        psError = "One or more required properties (FileFullPath and/or
FileInputName) not set"


End If
```

```
End Function


Public Property Get Error()

      Error = psError

End Property




' ----------------------------------------------------------------------

      Public Property Get ContentTypeOf(ByRef avKeyIndex)

            Dim lnIndex

            lnIndex = IndexOf(avKeyIndex)

            if lnIndex = -1 Then Exit Property

            ContentTypeOf = oFields(lnIndex).ContentType

      End Property



' ----------------------------------------------------------------------

      Private Sub Class_Terminate()

            Dim lnIndex

            For lnIndex = 0 To nFieldCount - 1

                  Set oFields(0) = Nothing

            Next

      End Sub

' ----------------------------------------------------------------------

      Private Sub Class_Initialize()
```

```
        Dim InBytes                    ' Bytes received from the client
        Dim InByteCount                ' Number of bytes received
        Dim InStartPosition            ' Position at which content begins
        Dim InEndPosition              ' Position at which content ends


        Dim IoDic                      ' Contains properties of each
                                           ' specific field
                                           ' Local dictionary object(s)
                                           ' to be appended to class-scope
                                           ' dictioary object.


        Dim InBoundaryBytes            ' Bytes contained within the current
boundary
        Dim InBoundaryStart            ' Position at wich the current boundary
begins
                                       ' within the InBytes binary data.
        Dim InBoundaryEnd              ' Position at wich the current boundary
ends
                                       ' within the InBytes binary data.
        Dim InDispositionPosition


        Dim IsFieldName                ' Name of the current field being parsed
from
                                       ' Binary Data
        Dim IsFileName                 ' Name of the file within the current
boundary
```

```
            Dim lnFileNamePosition        ' Location of file name within current
boundary

            Dim loField                   ' clsField Object

            Dim lsValue                      ' Value of the current field

            Dim lsContentType             ' ContentType of the binary file (MIME
Type)


            ' Initialize Fields

            nFieldCount = 0

            ReDim oFields(-1)


            ' Read the bytes (binary data) into memory

            lnByteCount = Request.TotalBytes

            lnBytes = Request.BinaryRead(lnByteCount)


            'Get the lnBoundaryBytes

            lnStartPosition = 1

            lnEndPosition = InstrB(lnStartPosition, lnBytes, CStrB(vbCr))


            If lnEndPosition >= lnStartPosition Then

                    lnBoundaryBytes = MidB(lnBytes, lnStartPosition,
lnEndPosition - lnStartPosition)

            End If


            lnBoundaryStart = InstrB(1, lnBytes, lnBoundaryBytes)
```

```
                ' Loop until the BoundaryBytes begin with "--"
            Do Until (lnBoundaryStart = InstrB(lnBytes, lnBoundaryBytes &
CStrB("--")))


                    ' All data within this boundary is stored within a local dictionary
                    ' to be appended to the class-scope dictionary.


                    ReDim Preserve oFields(nFieldCount)
                    nFieldCount = nFieldCount + 1


                    Set loField = New clsField


                    lnDispositionPosition = InstrB(lnBoundaryStart, lnBytes,
CStrB("Content-Disposition"))


                    ' Get an object name
                    lnStartPosition = InstrB(lnDispositionPosition, lnBytes,
CStrB("name=")) + 6
                    lnEndPosition = InstrB(lnStartPosition, lnBytes, CStrB(""""))
                    lsFieldName = CStrU(MidB(lnBytes, lnStartPosition,
lnEndPosition - lnStartPosition))
                    loField.FieldName = lsFieldName


                    ' Get the location fo the file name.
                    lnFileNamePosition = InstrB(lnBoundaryStart, lnBytes,
CStrB("filename="))
                    lnBoundaryEnd = InstrB(lnEndPosition, lnBytes,
lnBoundaryBytes)
```

```
'Test if object is a file

        If Not lnFileNamePosition = 0 And lnFileNamePosition <
lnBoundaryEnd Then


                ' Parse Filename

                lnStartPosition = lnFileNamePosition + 10

                lnEndPosition =  InstrB(lnStartPosition, lnBytes,
CStrB(""""))

                lsFileName =
CStrU(MidB(lnBytes,lnStartPosition,lnEndPosition-lnStartPosition))

                loField.FileName = lsFileName


                ' Parse Content-Type

                lnStartPosition =
InstrB(lnEndPosition,lnBytes,CStrB("Content-Type:")) + 14

                lnEndPosition =
InstrB(lnStartPosition,lnBytes,CStrB(vbCr))

                lsContentType =
CStrU(MidB(lnBytes,lnStartPosition,lnEndPosition-lnStartPosition))

                loField.ContentType = lsContentType


                ' Parse Content

                lnStartPosition = lnEndPosition + 4

                lnEndPosition =
InstrB(lnStartPosition,lnBytes,lnBoundaryBytes)-2

                lsValue = MidB(lnBytes,lnStartPosition,lnEndPosition-
lnStartPosition)

                loField.BinaryData = lsValue & CStrB(vbNull)
```

```
                loField.Length = LenB(lsValue)
        Else


                ' Parse Content
                lnStartPosition = InstrB(lnDispositionPosition, lnBytes,
CStrB(vbCr)) + 4

                lnEndPosition = InstrB(lnStartPosition, lnBytes,
lnBoundaryBytes) - 2
                lsValue =
CStrU(MidB(lnBytes,lnStartPosition,lnEndPosition-lnStartPosition))
                loField.Value = lsValue

                loField.Length = Len(lsValue)
        End If


        Set oFields(UBound(oFields)) = loField


        'Loop to next object
        lnBoundaryStart = InstrB(lnBoundaryStart +
LenB(lnBoundaryBytes), lnBytes, lnBoundaryBytes)


        Set loField = Nothing


    Loop


    End Sub
' ----------------------------------------------------------------------
    Private Function CStrU(ByRef psByteString)
```

```
            Dim lnLength

            Dim lnPosition

            lnLength = LenB(psByteString)

            For lnPosition = 1 To lnLength

                    CStrU = CStrU & Chr(AscB(MidB(psByteString, lnPosition, 1)))

            Next

        End Function
' -----------------------------------------------------------------------------

        Private Function CStrB(ByRef psUnicodeString)

            Dim lnLength

            Dim lnPosition

            lnLength = Len(psUnicodeString)

            For lnPosition = 1 To lnLength

                    CStrB = CStrB & ChrB(AscB(Mid(psUnicodeString, lnPosition,
1)))

            Next

        End Function
' -----------------------------------------------------------------------------

End Class
' -----------------------------------------------------------------------------

%>
```

CONTACT

```
<HTML>

<HEAD>

<TITLE>Contact us</TITLE>

</HEAD>

<BODY>

<HR>
```

Thanks for providing me a feedback. This site is intended for academic purposes, please do mail for future enhancements, proposals, or any services that you may find useful to add.

```
<PRE>

<P><B>Project information</P><B>

<P><B> Project   :</B> PJ 330<P>

<P><B> Year      :</B> August 2009<P>

<P><B> Course    :</B> BSc(Hons) Technology Management and Computing<P>

<P><B> University:</B> Portsmouth (collaborative Programme)<P>


</PRE>
```

```
<PRE>

<P>

<B>Email</B> <a href="mailto:cheers@intnet.mu">cheers@intnet.mu</a>. </P>




<b><font color="black">Table of contents: </b> <b><a
href="mapstoggle.html"><font color="red">MAPS</a> </b> <b><a
href="routes.asp"><font color="red">GPS & ROUTES</a></b> <b><font
color="white"><a href="viewprocess.asp"><font
color="red">INFORMATION</a></b> <b><font color="white"><a
href="enterforum.asp"><font color="red">FORUM & FAQS </a></b> <b><font
color="white"><a href="login.html"><font color="red">DATABASE
ADMINISTRATION </a></b> <b><font color="white"><a
href="contact.html"><font color="red">CONTACT US </a></b> <b><font
color="white"><a href="uopproject.html"><font color="red">RETURN TO MAIN
PAGE </a></b> </PRE>

<PRE>

<HR>


</BODY>


</HTML>
```

DELETE

```
<html>

<body>

<%

'create connection

set conn=Server.CreateObject("ADODB.Connection")

conn.Provider="Microsoft.Jet.OLEDB.4.0"

conn.Open
"c:\MemberSites\MemberSites_AspSpider_Ws\universityproject\database\gpsdatab
ase.mdb"

set rs=Server.CreateObject("ADODB.Recordset")

rs.open "SELECT * FROM records",conn

%>



<h2>Listing of Database</h2>

<table border="1" width="100%">

<tr>

<PRE>
```

```
<b><font color="black">Table of contents: </b> <b><a
href="mapstoggle.html"><font color="red">MAPS</a> </b> <b><a
href="routes.asp"><font color="red">GPS & ROUTES</a></b> <b><font
color="white"><a href="viewprocess.asp"><font
color="red">INFORMATION</a></b> <b><font color="white"><a
href="enterforum.asp"><font color="red">FORUM & FAQS </a></b> <b><font
color="white"><a href="login.html"><font color="red">DATABASE
ADMINISTRATION </a></b> <b><font color="white"><a
href="contact.html"><font color="red">CONTACT US </a></b> <b><font
```

color="white"><a href="uopproject.html"><font color="red">RETURN TO MAIN
PAGE </a></b> </PRE>

<PRE>

```asp
<%
for each x in rs.Fields
  response.write("<th>" & ucase(x.name) & "</th>")
next
%>
</tr>
<% do until rs.EOF %>
<tr>
<form method="post" action="deleteprocess.asp">
<%
for each x in rs.Fields
  if x.name="name" then%>
    <td>
    <input type="submit" name="name" value="<%=x.value%>">
    </td>
  <%else%>
    <td><%Response.Write(x.value)%></td>
  <%end if
next
%>
</form>
<%rs.MoveNext%>
```

```
</tr>

<%

loop

conn.close

%>

</table>

</body>

</html>
```

DELETE PROCESS

```
<html>

<body>


<h2>Delete Record</h2>

<%


'create connection

set conn=Server.CreateObject("ADODB.Connection")

conn.Provider="Microsoft.Jet.OLEDB.4.0"

conn.Open
"c:\MemberSites\MemberSites_AspSpider_Ws\universityproject\database\gpsdatab
ase.mdb"


cid=Request.Form("name")


if Request.form("name")="" then

  set rs=Server.CreateObject("ADODB.Recordset")
```

```
rs.open "SELECT * FROM forum WHERE name='" & cid & "'",conn
%>
<form method="post" action="demo_delete.asp">
<table>
<%for each x in rs.Fields%>
<tr>
<td><%=x.name%></td>
<td><input name="<%=x.name%>" value="<%=x.value%>"></td>
<%next%>
</tr>
</table>
<br /><br />
<input type="submit" value="Delete record">
</form>
<%
else
  sql="DELETE FROM forum"
  sql=sql & " WHERE name='" & cid & "'"
  on error resume next
  conn.Execute sql
  if err<>0 then
    response.write("No update permissions!")
  else
    response.write("Record " & cid & " was deleted!")
  end if
end if
```

```
conn.close

%>


</body>

</html>
```

ENTERDATA

```html
<html>
<head>
<title> Enter data </title>
<script type="text/javascript">
<!--
function validate()
{
  if(document.form.name.value=="")
  {
   alert("Name is missing");
   return false;
  }


  if(document.form.type.address.length<4)
  {
   alert("Address too short");
   return false;
  }
```

```
if(document.form.type.tel.length<4)

{

alert("invalid phone num");

return false;

}


if(document.form.type.lat.length<4)

{

alert("Latitude lacks precision");

return false;

}


if(document.form.type.lng.length<4)

{

alert("Longitude lacks precision");

return false;

}


if(document.form.type.type.length<3)

{

alert("Too short type, enter either hotel, restaurant, or Fuel");

return false;

}


else

{
```

```
  return true;

  }

}

//-->

</script>

</head>

<body>

<form name="form" method="post" action="saveprocess.asp">

<PRE>

<br>Name        : <input type="text" name="name" maxlength="45"> </br>

<br>Address     : <input type="text" name="address" maxlength="45"> </br>

<br>Telephone   : <input type="text" name="tel" maxlength="45"> </br>

<br>Latitude    : <input type="text" name="lat" maxlength="45"> </br>

<br>Longitude   : <input type="text" name="lng" maxlength="45"> </br>

<br>Region      : <input type="text" name="region" maxlength="45"> </br>

<br>Type        : <input type="text" name="type" maxlength="45"> </br>

<br><input type="submit" name="Save" value="Submit" onClick="return
validate();"> </br>

</PRE>

<PRE>




<b><font color="black">Table of contents: </b> <b><a
href="mapstoggle.html"><font color="red">MAPS</a> </b> <b><a
href="routes.asp"><font color="red">GPS & ROUTES</a></b> <b><font
color="white"><a href="viewprocess.asp"><font
color="red">INFORMATION</a></b> <b><font color="white"><a
```

```
href="enterforum.asp"><font color="red">FORUM & FAQS </a></b> <b><font
color="white"><a href="login.html"><font color="red">DATABASE
ADMINISTRATION </a></b> <b><font color="white"><a
href="contact.html"><font color="red">CONTACT US </a></b> <b><font
color="white"><a href="uopproject.html"><font color="red">RETURN TO MAIN
PAGE </a></b> </PRE>

<PRE>


</form>

</body>

</html>
```

ENTERFORUM

```
<html>
<head>
<title> View forum comments </title>
<script type="text/javascript">
<!--
function validate()
{
 if(document.form.name.value=="")
 {
  alert("Name is missing");
  return false;
 }
 if(document.form.type.value.length<4)
 {
  alert("Not enough comments entered");
  return false;
 }
 else
 {
  return true;
 }
}
//-->
</script>
</head>
```

```html
<body>

<form name="form" method="post" action="forumprocess.asp">

<PRE>

<br>Name    : <input type="text" name="name" maxlength="45"> </br>

<br>Email   : <input type="text" name="email" maxlength="45"> </br>

<br>Notes   : <input type="text" name="notes" maxlength="45"> </br>

<input type="submit" name="Save" value="Submit" onClick="return validate();">


<INPUT type='button' name='Button1' value='View forum notes!'
onclick="window.location='http://aspspider.ws/universityproject/recordsetforum.as
p'">

<PRE>




<b><font color="black">Table of contents: </b> <b><a
href="mapstoggle.html"><font color="red">MAPS</a> </b> <b><a
href="routes.asp"><font color="red">GPS & ROUTES</a></b> <b><font
color="white"><a href="viewprocess.asp"><font
color="red">INFORMATION</a></b> <b><font color="white"><a
href="enterforum.asp"><font color="red">FORUM & FAQS </a></b> <b><font
color="white"><a href="login.html"><font color="red">DATABASE
ADMINISTRATION </a></b> <b><font color="white"><a
href="contact.html"><font color="red">CONTACT US </a></b> <b><font
color="white"><a href="uopproject.html"><font color="red">RETURN TO MAIN
PAGE </a></b> </PRE>

<PRE>

</form>

</body>

</html>
```

FORUMPROCESS

```
<%

Dim Conn

Dim Rs

Dim sql


'create connection

Set Conn = Server.CreateObject("ADODB.Connection")

Set Rs = Server.CreateObject("ADODB.Recordset")

Conn.Provider="Microsoft.Jet.OLEDB.4.0"


conn.Open
"c:\MemberSites\MemberSites_AspSpider_Ws\universityproject\database\gpsdatab
ase.mdb"


sql= "SELECT name, email, notes FROM forum;"

'Set the lock and cursor type

Rs.CursorType = 2

Rs.LockType = 3

Rs.Open sql, Conn     'Open the recordset with sql query

Rs.AddNew 'Prepare the database to add a new record and add

Rs.Fields("name") = Request.Form("name")

Rs.Fields("email") = Request.Form("email")

Rs.Fields("notes") = Request.Form("notes")


Rs.Update    'Save the update
```

```
Rs.Close

Set Rs = Nothing

Set Conn = Nothing

%>
```

GPSLOADMODULE

```
<html>

<body>

<p>GPS read module:</p>


<%

Dim x



xmlFile = Server.MapPath("markerdata2.txt")

Set fs=Server.CreateObject("Scripting.FileSystemObject")


'rename file uploaded

fso.MoveFile "GPX.gpx",
"c:\MemberSites\MemberSites_AspSpider_Ws\universityproject\database\gpx.txt"

    set fso = Nothing



set objFSO  = Server.CreateObject( "Scripting.FileSystemObject" )

If Not objFSO.FileExists( xmlFile ) Then objFSO.CreateTextFile( xmlFile )

set objWrite = objFSO.OpenTextFile( xmlFile, 2 )

objWrite.WriteLine("<?xml version=""1.0"" encoding=""ISO-8859-1""?>")
```

```
objWrite.WriteLine("<marker>")


x=0;


Do while EOF
x=x+1;
Set f=fs.OpenTextFile(Server.MapPath("gpx.txt"), "x")


if (f.ReadLine)= ("lat")
then
objWrite.WriteLine(tb & "<point>")
   objWrite.WriteLine(tb & tb & "<lat>" & rs("latin") & "</lat>")
   objWrite.WriteLine(tb & "</point>")
else
if (f.ReadLine)= ("lng")
then
objWrite.WriteLine(tb & "<point>")
   objWrite.WriteLine(tb & tb & "<lng>" & rs("lng") & "</lng>")
   objWrite.WriteLine(tb & "</point>")


Wend
f.Close


Set f=Nothing
Set fs=Nothing
```

```
fso.MoveFile "markerdata2.txt",
"c:\MemberSites\MemberSites_AspSpider_Ws\universityproject\database\markerda
ta2.xml"

    set fso = Nothing




%>




</body>

</html>
```

LABELLEDMARKER

/*

* LabeledMarker Class, v1.2

*

* Copyright 2007 Mike Purvis (http://uwmike.com)

*

* Licensed under the Apache License, Version 2.0 (the "License");

* you may not use this file except in compliance with the License.

* You may obtain a copy of the License at

*   http://www.apache.org/licenses/LICENSE-2.0

* Unless required by applicable law or agreed to in writing, software

* distributed under the License is distributed on an "AS IS" BASIS,

* WITHOUT WARRANTIES OR CONDITIONS OF ANY KIND, either express or implied.

* See the License for the specific language governing permissions and

* limitations under the License.

*

* This class extends the Maps API's standard GMarker class with the ability

* to support markers with textual labels. Please see articles here:

*

*   http://googlemapsbook.com/2007/01/22/extending-gmarker/

*   http://googlemapsbook.com/2007/03/06/clickable-labeledmarker/

*/

/**

 * Constructor for LabeledMarker, which picks up on strings from the GMarker

```
* options array, and then calls the GMarker constructor.
*
* @param {GLatLng} latlng
* @param {GMarkerOptions} Named optional arguments:
*   opt_opts.labelText {String} text to place in the overlay div.
*   opt_opts.labelClass {String} class to use for the overlay div.
*     (default "LabeledMarker_markerLabel")
*   opt_opts.labelOffset {GSize} label offset, the x- and y-distance between
*     the marker's latlng and the upper-left corner of the text div.
*/
function LabeledMarker(latlng, opt_opts){
  this.latlng_ = latlng;
  this.opts_ = opt_opts;

  this.labelText_ = opt_opts.labelText || "";
  this.labelClass_ = opt_opts.labelClass || "LabeledMarker_markerLabel";
  this.labelOffset_ = opt_opts.labelOffset || new GSize(0, 0);

  this.clickable_ = opt_opts.clickable || true;
  this.title_ = opt_opts.title || "";
  this.labelVisibility_ = true;

  if (opt_opts.draggable) {
    // This version of LabeledMarker doesn't support dragging.
    opt_opts.draggable = false;
  }
```

```
  GMarker.apply(this, arguments);

};

// It's a limitation of JavaScript inheritance that we can't conveniently

// inherit from GMarker without having to run its constructor. In order for

// the constructor to run, it requires some dummy GLatLng.

LabeledMarker.prototype = new GMarker(new GLatLng(0, 0));


/**

 * Is called by GMap2's addOverlay method. Creates the text div and adds it

 * to the relevant parent div.

 *

 * @param {GMap2} map the map that has had this labeledmarker added to it.

 */

LabeledMarker.prototype.initialize = function(map) {

  // Do the GMarker constructor first.

  GMarker.prototype.initialize.apply(this, arguments);


  this.map_ = map;

  this.div_ = document.createElement("div");

  this.div_.className = this.labelClass_;

  this.div_.innerHTML = this.labelText_;

  this.div_.style.position = "absolute";

  this.div_.style.cursor = "pointer";

  this.div_.title = this.title_;

  map.getPane(G_MAP_MARKER_PANE).appendChild(this.div_);
```

```
if (this.clickable_) {

  /**

   * Creates a closure for passing events through to the source marker

   * This is located in here to avoid cluttering the global namespace.

   * The downside is that the local variables from initialize() continue

   * to occupy space on the stack.

   *

   * @param {Object} object to receive event trigger.

   * @param {GEventListener} event to be triggered.

   */
  function newEventPassthru(obj, event) {

    return function() {

      GEvent.trigger(obj, event);

    };

  }

  // Pass through events fired on the text div to the marker.

  var eventPassthrus = ['click', 'dblclick', 'mousedown', 'mouseup', 'mouseover',
'mouseout'];

    for(var i = 0; i < eventPassthrus.length; i++) {

    var name = eventPassthrus[i];

    GEvent.addDomListener(this.div_, name, newEventPassthru(this, name));

    }

  }

};

/**

 * Call the redraw() handler in GMarker and our our redrawLabel() function.
```

*

* @param {Boolean} force will be true when pixel coordinates need to be recomputed.

*/

LabeledMarker.prototype.redraw = function(force) {

  GMarker.prototype.redraw.apply(this, arguments);

  this.redrawLabel_();

};

/**

* Moves the text div based on current projection and zoom level.

*/

LabeledMarker.prototype.redrawLabel_ = function() {

  // Calculate the DIV coordinates of two opposite corners of our bounds to

  // get the size and position of our rectangle

  var p = this.map_.fromLatLngToDivPixel(this.latlng_);

  var z = GOverlay.getZIndex(this.latlng_.lat());

  // Now position our div based on the div coordinates of our bounds

  this.div_.style.left = (p.x + this.labelOffset_.width) + "px";

  this.div_.style.top = (p.y + this.labelOffset_.height) + "px";

  this.div_.style.zIndex = z; // in front of the marker

};

/**

* Remove the text div from the map pane, destroy event passthrus, and calls the

* default remove() handler in GMarker.

*/

```
LabeledMarker.prototype.remove = function() {

GEvent.clearInstanceListeners(this.div_);

if (this.div_.outerHTML) {

  this.div_.outerHTML = ""; //prevent pseudo-leak in IE

}

if (this.div_.parentNode) {

  this.div_.parentNode.removeChild(this.div_);

}

this.div_ = null;

GMarker.prototype.remove.apply(this, arguments);

};

/**

* Return a copy of this overlay, for the parent Map to duplicate itself in full. This

* is part of the Overlay interface and is used, for example, to copy everything in the

* main view into the mini-map.

*/

LabeledMarker.prototype.copy = function() {

  return new LabeledMarker(this.latlng_, this.opts_);

};




/**

* Shows the marker, and shows label if it wasn't hidden. Note that this function

* triggers the event GMarker.visibilitychanged in case the marker is currently hidden.

*/
```

```
LabeledMarker.prototype.show = function() {
  GMarker.prototype.show.apply(this, arguments);
  if (this.labelVisibility_) {
    this.showLabel();
  } else {
    this.hideLabel();
  }
};
```

```
/**
 * Hides the marker and label if it is currently visible. Note that this function
 * triggers the event GMarker.visibilitychanged in case the marker is currently
 * visible.
 */
LabeledMarker.prototype.hide = function() {
  GMarker.prototype.hide.apply(this, arguments);
  this.hideLabel();
};
/**
 * Repositions label and marker when setLatLng is called.
 */
LabeledMarker.prototype.setLatLng = function(latlng) {
  this.latlng_ = latlng;
  GMarker.prototype.setLatLng.apply(this, arguments);
  this.redrawLabel_();
```

```
};


/**

 * Sets the visibility of the label, which will be respected during show/hides.

 * If marker is visible when set, it will show or hide label appropriately.

 */

LabeledMarker.prototype.setLabelVisibility = function(visibility) {

  this.labelVisibility_ = visibility;

  if (!this.isHidden()) { // Marker showing, make visible change

    if (this.labelVisibility_) {

      this.showLabel();

    } else {

      this.hideLabel();

    }

  }

};
/**

 * Returns whether label visibility is set on.

 * @return {Boolean}

 */

LabeledMarker.prototype.getLabelVisibility = function() {

  return this.labelVisibility_;

};


/** * Hides the label of the marker.
```

```
 */

LabeledMarker.prototype.hideLabel = function() {

  this.div_.style.visibility = 'hidden';

};




/**

 * Shows the label of the marker.

 */

LabeledMarker.prototype.showLabel = function() {

  this.div_.style.visibility = 'visible';

};
```

LINKS

```
<HTML>

<HEAD>

<TITLE></TITLE>

<META name="description" content="">

<META name="keywords" content="">

<META name="generator" content="CuteHTML">

</HEAD>

<BODY BGCOLOR="#FFFFFF" TEXT="#000000" LINK="#0000FF"
VLINK="#800080">


Useful links of websites in mauritius



<pre>

<a href="http://www.orange.mu/"><font color="black">Orange Portal-
Telecommunication</a>

<a href="http://www.emtel-ltd.com/"><font color="black">Emtel Portal-
Telecommunication</a>

<a
href="http://www.gov.mu/portal/site/Mainhomepage/menuitem.cc515006ac7521ae3
a9dbea5e2b521ca/"><font color="black">Government of mauritius</a>

<a href="http://http://http://www.mcci.org/"><font color="black">Mauritius
chamber of commerce and inustries</a>

        </pre>

</BODY>

</HTML>
```

LOGIN

```
<%

username = replace(request.form("txtUsername"),"'","''")

password = replace(request.form("txtPassword"),"'","''")

'create connection

Set Conn = Server.CreateObject("ADODB.Connection")

Set Rs = Server.CreateObject("ADODB.Recordset")

Conn.Provider="Microsoft.Jet.OLEDB.4.0"

conn.Open
"c:\MemberSites\MemberSites_AspSpider_Ws\universityproject\database\gpsdatab
ase.mdb"

sqlLogin = "select * from login where [username] = '" & username & "' and
[password] = '" & password & "'"

rs.Open sqlLogin, conn

if rs.EOF then

        response.write "username|password incorrect. Click back to try again"

else

        session("username") = rs("Username")

        response.redirect "admin.html"

end if

rs.close

conn.close

set rs = nothing

set conn = nothing

%>
```

LOGIN HTML

```
<form name="frmLogin" action="login.asp" method="post">
```

```html
<pre>

User:    <input type="text" name="txtUsername" />

Password: <input type="password" name="txtPassword" />

       <input type="submit" value="Login" />

<pre>

</form>
```

MAPSTOGGLE

```html
<!DOCTYPE html PUBLIC "-//W3C//DTD XHTML 1.0 Strict//EN"

  "http://www.w3.org/TR/xhtml1/DTD/xhtml1-strict.dtd">

<html xmlns="http://www.w3.org/1999/xhtml">

 <head>

  <meta http-equiv="content-type" content="text/html; charset=utf-8"/>

   <title>Maps:interesting spots in mauritius</title>

<script
src="http://maps.google.com/maps?file=api&amp;v=2&amp;key=ABQIAAAAFsN9
cRz_z1FbAPiZ8UEGmRScZl2UBoZk3KAefkbgN5dmiuoq5xQRK2eHF8-6qh2-
bsTJvssCSqsINQ" type="text/javascript"></script>

<script src="labelledmarker.js"></script>

  <script type="text/javascript">



 var iconGreen = new GIcon();

  iconGreen.image = 'http://gmaps-
samples.googlecode.com/svn/trunk/markers/circular/greencirclemarker.png';

  iconGreen.shadow = '';

  iconGreen.iconSize = new GSize(32, 32);

  iconGreen.shadowSize = new GSize(22, 20);
```

```
iconGreen.iconAnchor = new GPoint(16, 16);

iconGreen.infoWindowAnchor = new GPoint(5, 1);


var iconRed = new GIcon();

iconRed.image = 'images/redCircle.png';

iconRed.shadow = '';

iconRed.iconSize = new GSize(32, 32);

iconRed.shadowSize = new GSize(22, 20);

iconRed.iconAnchor = new GPoint(16, 16);

iconRed.infoWindowAnchor = new GPoint(5, 1);



    var iconYellow = new GIcon();

iconYellow.image = 'http://gmaps-
samples.googlecode.com/svn/trunk/markers/circular/yellowcirclemarker.png';

iconYellow.shadow = '';

iconYellow.iconSize = new GSize(32, 32);

iconYellow.shadowSize = new GSize(22, 20);

iconYellow.iconAnchor = new GPoint(16, 16);

iconYellow.infoWindowAnchor = new GPoint(5, 1);


var iconBlue = new GIcon();

iconBlue.image = 'http://gmaps-
samples.googlecode.com/svn/trunk/markers/circular/bluecirclemarker.png';

iconBlue.shadow = '';

iconBlue.iconSize = new GSize(32, 32);

iconBlue.shadowSize = new GSize(22, 20);
```

```
iconBlue.iconAnchor = new GPoint(16, 16);

iconBlue.infoWindowAnchor = new GPoint(5, 1);


var customIcons = [];

customIcons["restaurant"] = iconBlue;

customIcons["hotel"] = iconRed;

    customIcons["fuel"] = iconYellow;

    customIcons["hospital"] = iconGreen;

var markerGroups = { "restaurant": [], "hotel": [], "fuel" : [], "hospital" : [] };


function load() {

  if (GBrowserIsCompatible()) {

    var map = new GMap2(document.getElementById("map"));


    map.setCenter(new GLatLng(-20.266451, 57.603011), 10);

    document.getElementById("restaurantCheckbox").checked = true;

    document.getElementById("hotelCheckbox").checked = true;

        document.getElementById("fuelCheckbox").checked = true;

        document.getElementById("hospitalCheckbox").checked = true;

    document.getElementById("labelsCheckbox").checked = true;
```

```
GDownloadUrl("markerdata.xml", function(data) {

    var xml = GXml.parse(data);

    var markers = xml.documentElement.getElementsByTagName("marker");

        for (var i = 0; i < markers.length; i++) {

      var name = markers[i].getAttribute("name");

      var label = markers[i].getAttribute("label");

      var address = markers[i].getAttribute("address");

      var type = markers[i].getAttribute("type");

      var point = new GLatLng(parseFloat(markers[i].getAttribute("lat")),

                    parseFloat(markers[i].getAttribute("lng")));

    var marker = createMarker(point, name, label, address, type);

    map.addOverlay(marker);

  }

   });

  }

 }



 function createMarker(point, name, label, address, type) {

    var marker = new LabeledMarker(point, {icon: customIcons[type], labelText:
label, labelOffset: new GSize(-6, -10)});

   markerGroups[type].push(marker);

   var html = "<b>" + name + "</b> <br/>" + address;

   GEvent.addListener(marker, 'click', function() {

    marker.openInfoWindowHtml(html);

   });
```

```
    return marker;
  }
  function toggleGroup(type) {
    for (var i = 0; i < markerGroups[type].length; i++) {
      var marker = markerGroups[type][i];
      if (marker.isHidden()) {
        marker.show();
      } else {
        marker.hide();
      }
    }
  }



  function toggleLabels() {
    var showLabels = document.getElementById("labelsCheckbox").checked;
    for (groupName in markerGroups) {
      for (var i = 0; i < markerGroups[groupName].length; i++) {
        var marker = markerGroups[groupName][i];
        marker.setLabelVisibility(showLabels);
      }
    }
  }


  //]]>
</script>
```

```
</head>
```

```
<body style="font-family:Arial, sans serif" onload="load()"
onunload="GUnload()">
```

```
<input type="checkbox" id="labelsCheckbox" onclick="toggleLabels()"
CHECKED /> Show Labels
```

```
<br/><P><B> Welcome to the maps page.</P></B>
```

```
<PRE>
```

```
<P> This part, shows points uploaded, from a database. Our administrator updates
regularly interesting spots to see.
```

At this stage only a few togglers are available: Hotels around the coastal regions

                                  : Fuelling places(caltex stations)

                                  : Restaurants

                                  : Hospitals   </P>

Instructions:

Click on Show labels to view labelling

Toggle Hotels, Fuelling, Restaurants, if you wish to see only a category

Click on the spots, to get more information(eg:location of spot)

Left click on mouse, to drag around & double-click to get more details

```
</PRE>
```

```
   <div id="map" style="float:left; width: 500px; height: 500px; border: 1px solid
black"></div>

   <div id="sidebar" style="float:left; width: 120px; height: 100px; border: 1px
solid black">

<input type="checkbox" id="restaurantCheckbox"
onclick="toggleGroup('restaurant')" CHECKED />

   Restaurants

   <br/>


<input type="checkbox" id="hotelCheckbox" onclick="toggleGroup('hotel')"
CHECKED/>

   Hotel

        <br/>
<input type="checkbox" id="fuelCheckbox" onclick="toggleGroup('fuel')"
CHECKED/>

   Fuel

        <br/>
<input type="checkbox" id="hospitalCheckbox" onclick="toggleGroup('hospital')"
CHECKED/>

   Hospital


   </div>

<PRE>
```

```
<P><b><font color="black">Table of contents </p></b>


<b><a href="mapstoggle.html"><font color="red">MAPS</a></b>
<b><a href="routes.asp"><font color="red">GPS & ROUTES</a>
<b><font color="white"><a href="viewprocess.asp"><font
color="red">INFORMATION</a></b>
<b><font color="white"><a href="enterforum.asp"><font color="red">FORUM &
FAQS </a></b>
<b><font color="white"><a href="login.html"><font color="red">DATABASE
ADMINISTRATION </a></b>
<b><font color="white"><a href="contact.html"><font color="red">CONTACT US
</a></b>
<b><font color="white"><a href="uopproject.html"><font color="red">RETURN
TO MAIN PAGE </a></b>
<pre>
  </body>
</html>
```

MARKERDATA

```
<markers>
<marker name="Chez Patrick" address="Royal Road, Mahebourg" lat="-
20.411891" lng="57.706032" type="restaurant" />
<marker name="Le gris gris" address="Souillac" lat="-20.51868" lng="57.528534"
type="restaurant" />
<marker name="Choice food palace" address="Route St Paul, Phoenix" lat="-
20.287317" lng="57.50776" type="restaurant" />
<marker name="Red lobster" address="Comlone branch road, nouvelle france"
lat="-20.374038" lng="57.562866" type="restaurant" />
```

```
<marker name="Debonnairs pizza" address="Port Louis" lat="-20.163288"
lng="57.503901" type="restaurant" />

<marker name="Domaine des pailles " address="Pailles, next to conference centre"
lat="-20.202199" lng="57.48381" type="restaurant" />

<marker name="Don camillo" address="on the north coast" lat="-20.015613"
lng="572823" type="restaurant" />

<marker name="King dragon" address="Royal road, quatres bornes" lat="-
20.27049" lng="57.474976" type="restaurant" />

<marker name="Luigi italien" address="on the north coast" lat="-20.009645"
lng="57.582006" type="restaurant" />

<marker name="Mc Donald" address="Next to harbour front, Port Louis" lat="-
20.164617" lng="57.49827" type="restaurant" />

<marker name="Restaurant domaine moulin au vent" address="" lat="-20.023436"
lng="57.628226" type="restaurant" />


<marker name="Le pescatore " address="Royal road, trou aux biches" lat="-
20.030613" lng="57.547159" type="restaurant" />

<marker name="Salam bombay" address="Royal road, moka" lat="-20.226281"
lng="57.506218" type="restaurant" />

<marker name="Hotel ambre" address="east coast" lat="-20.190357"
lng="57.774868" type="hotel" />

<marker name="Hotel casuarina" address="in the north" lat="-20.039483"
lng="57.542953" type="hotel" />

<marker name="Club mediterranee" address="Royal road, pointe aux cannoniers"
lat="-19.989643" lng="57.590675" type="hotel" />

<marker name="Le prince maurice" address="East coast" lat="-20.1633449"
lng="57.745686" type="hotel" />

<marker name="Hotel casuarina" address="in the north" lat="-20.039483"
lng="57.542953" type="hotel" />

<marker name="Hilton" address="East coast" lat="-20.29259" lng="57.363095"
type="hotel" />
```

```
<marker name="Le tropical" address="East coast" lat="-20.253984"
lng="57.797871" type="hotel" />

<marker name="Tarisa resoirt" address="Choisy" lat="-20.006288"
lng="57.5516638" type="hotel" />

<marker name="Le preskil" address="On the south coast" lat="-20.408834"
lng="57.710066" type="hotel" />

<marker name="Hotel Tamassa" address="On the south coast" lat="-20.511606"
lng="57.423134" type="hotel" />


</markers>
```

MYALBUM

```
<!DOCTYPE html PUBLIC "-//W3C//DTD XHTML 1.0 Transitional//EN"
"http://www.w3.org/TR/xhtml1/DTD/xhtml1-transitional.dtd">

<html xmlns="http://www.w3.org/1999/xhtml" xml:lang="en" lang="en">

<head>

<meta http-equiv="Content-Type" content="text/html; charset=UTF-8" />

<title>photos</title>

</head>

<body bgcolor="#FFFFFF">

<p> <p>

<style type="text/css">

<!--

.style1 {

    color: #006633;

    font-weight: bold;

}

-->

</style>
```

```html
<!-- saved from url=(0013)about:internet -->
<table align="center" border="0" cellpadding=0 cellspacing=0>
  <tr>
    <td align="center">photos</td>
  </tr>
  <tr><td align="center"><br /></td></tr>
  <tr>
    <td align="center">
        <object classid="clsid:d27cdb6e-ae6d-11cf-96b8-444553540000"
codebase="http://fpdownload.macromedia.com/pub/shockwave/cabs/flash/swflash.c
ab#version=6,0,0,0" width="800" height="630" id="tech" align="middle">
            <param name="allowScriptAccess" value="sameDomain" />
            <param name="movie" value="myalbum.swf" />
            <param name="quality" value="high" />
            <embed src="myalbum.swf" quality="high" width="800" height="630"
name="tech" align="middle" allowScriptAccess="sameDomain"
type="application/x-shockwave-flash"
pluginspage="http://www.macromedia.com/go/getflashplayer" />
        </object>
    </td>
  </tr>
  <tr>
    <td align="center" ><br />
      Created by <a href="http://www.photo-flash-maker.com"
target="_blank">AnvSoft Photo Flash Maker</a>
    </td>
  </tr>
</table>
```

```
</body>

</html>
```

RECORDSETFORUM

```
<%@LANGUAGE=VBScript%>

<%

' Define variables

dim recordsonpage, requestrecords, offset, allrecords, hiddenrecords, showrecords,
lastrecord, recordcounter, pagelist, pagelistcounter




' DB connection

dim Conn

Set Conn = Server.CreateObject("ADODB.Connection")

Set Rs = Server.CreateObject("ADODB.Recordset")

Conn.Provider="Microsoft.Jet.OLEDB.4.0"

Conn.Open
"c:\MemberSites\MemberSites_AspSpider_Ws\universityproject\database\gpsdatab
ase.mdb"




' records per page

recordsonpage = 5


' count all records

allrecords = 0

set rs = Conn.Execute("SELECT * FROM forum")

do until rs.EOF
```

```
allrecords = allrecords + 1

rs.movenext

loop


' if offset is zero then the first page will be loaded

offset = request.querystring("offset")

if offset = 0 OR offset = "" then

  requestrecords = 0

else

  requestrecords = requestrecords + offset

end if


' opens database

set rs = Conn.Execute("SELECT * FROM forum ORDER BY name")


' reads first records (offset)

hiddenrecords = requestrecords

do until hiddenrecords = 0 OR rs.EOF

  hiddenrecords = hiddenrecords - 1

  rs.movenext

  if rs.EOF then

    lastrecord = 1

  end if

loop

%>
```

```
<html>
 <head>
  <title>view records</title>
  <meta http-equiv="author" content="ny">
 </head>
<body>


<table cellspacing="2" cellpadding="2" border="1" width="400">


<%
' prints records in the table
showrecords = recordsonpage
recordcounter = requestrecords
do until showrecords = 0 OR rs.EOF
recordcounter = recordcounter + 1
%>


 <tr>
  <td><b><% = recordcounter %></b></td>
  <td><% = rs("name") %></td>
  <td><% = rs("email") %></td>
<td><% = rs("notes") %></td>
</tr>


<%
 showrecords = showrecords - 1
```

```
  rs.movenext
  if rs.EOF then
    lastrecord = 1
  end if
loop
%>
```

```
</table>
```

```
<p>
```

```
<table cellspacing="2" cellpadding="2" border="1" width="400">
 <tr>
  <td><% if requestrecords <> 0 then %><a href="recordsetforum.asp?offset=<% =
requestrecords - recordsonpage %>">Prev Page</a><% else %>Prev Page<% end if
%></td>
  <td><% if lastrecord <> 1 then %>   <a href="recordsetforum.asp?offset=<% =
requestrecords + recordsonpage %>">Next Page</a><% else %>Next Page<% end
if %></td>
 </tr>
 <tr>
  <td colspan="2">pagelist:
<%
pagelist = 0
pagelistcounter = 0
do until pagelist > allrecords
  pagelistcounter = pagelistcounter + 1
```

```
%>

<a href="recordsetforum.asp?offset=<% = pagelist %>"><% = pagelistcounter
%></a>

<%

  pagelist = pagelist + recordsonpage

loop

%>

  </td>

 </tr>

</table>


<%

' Closes connection

rs.close

Conn.close

%>
```

</body>
</html>

ROUTES

```
<!DOCTYPE html PUBLIC "-//W3C//DTD XHTML 1.0 Strict//EN"
"http://www.w3.org/TR/xhtml1/DTD/xhtml1-strict.dtd">

<html xmlns="http://www.w3.org/1999/xhtml" xmlns:v="urn:schemas-microsoft-
com:vml">



<head>
<meta http-equiv="content-type" content="text/html; charset=iso-8859-1"/>
<!--#include file="clsUpload.asp"-->
<title>GPS and Routes</title>


<link rel="stylesheet" type="text/css" href="/mapStyle.css" />


<style>
.wText {
     border: 1px solid gray;
     padding: 5px;
     margin: 2px;
     font: normal 10px verdana;
     width: 200px;
}
#map {
     width: 800px;
     height:600px;
```

```
}

</style>


<script type="text/javascript" src="/key.js"></script>


<script type="text/javascript">
        var scriptTag = '<' + 'script
src="http://maps.google.com/maps?file=api&v=2&key=ABQIAAAAFsN9cRz_z1Fb
APiZ8UEGmRScZl2UBoZk3KAefkbgN5dmiuoq5xQRK2eHF8-6qh2-
bsTJvssCSqsINQ" type="text/javascript">'+'<'+'/script>';

        document.write(scriptTag);
</script>


<script type="text/javascript">
//<![CDATA[


var routePoints = new Array();

var routeMarkers = new Array();

var routeOverlays = new Array();

var map;

var totalDistance = 0.0;

var lineIx = 0;


var baseIcon = new GIcon();

baseIcon.iconSize=new GSize(16,16);
```

```
baseIcon.iconAnchor=new GPoint(8,8);

baseIcon.infoWindowAnchor=new GPoint(10,0);


var yellowIcon = (new GIcon(baseIcon, "yellowSquare.png", null, ""));

var greenIcon = (new GIcon(baseIcon, "greenCircle.png", null, ""));

var redIcon = (new GIcon(baseIcon, "redCircle.png", null, ""));

var orangeIcon = (new GIcon(baseIcon, "orangeCircle.png", null, ""));

var blueIcon = (new GIcon(baseIcon, "blueCircle.png", null, ""));

var violetIcon = (new GIcon(baseIcon, "blackCircle.png", null, ""));

function load() {

  if (GBrowserIsCompatible()) {

      var centerPoint = new GLatLng(-20.202924,57.571106);


      map = new
GMap2(document.getElementById("map"),{draggableCursor:"crosshair"});

      map.setCenter(centerPoint, 10);

      getMapcenter();


      map.addControl(new GMapTypeControl());

      map.addControl(new GScaleControl());

      map.addControl(new GLargeMapControl());



      map.enableContinuousZoom();

      GEvent.addListener(map, "moveend", getMapcenter);

      GEvent.addListener(map, "click", mapClick);
```

```
// ======== Add a map overview ==========

    var ovcontrol = new GOverviewMapControl(new GSize(120,120));

    map.addControl(ovcontrol);
```

```
return;

var pl = new GPolyline.fromEncoded({

  color: "#0000ff",

  weight: 4,

  opacity: 0.8,

  points:
"_gkxEr}lvNcBwBoAoA{Jg@cBcBoA{@S?uBoA}@wBS_DbBwhATg@c[sDiT}\\g
@i@{@S{@{@ScBRSnAg@SoAS{Eg@kCkClH?nAoF`LQRU{E~CgJ?g@jCqNrNc
Gz@?zJyBf@y@~CmC{@zJ?f@mAnA?f@x@z@bBR~HsIRe@jClKRz@`Dh@`Bd
@vBRnF_DRSg@S?wBpFcGd@SScBwBvB{@T_D~Cg@?oA`B{@R{E~CqD{EUgJ
wB{@nAoA?kChJrIdJaBz@i@f@_DdBf@dEgEnFcGoP_N{@SeTvBqKoA{J_SsDoF
?_Df@{@vB_XoAoPbLoZrDcBy@{EmC_D{ToAy@g@?_DlAgEgEcLg@g@qDnAq
AkR_DyJy@i@mC?g@{@}CqNi@i@_ISoK_g@g@{@{EiCiCd@g@z@yGfOwBnA
oARyJ_DuDRoAg@_D_IoKyEcGk\\gOx@cGy@{@}@sI_DcGgEwLbBuBRmCe@{J
gOS}Jy@{@kHcBy[_]gEmPnA}Ef@g@vGwBgEa[rDqPlh@w[hMoFzJ{J~HwL{@_
DoAkCcGwBuBgJyBoA_SfJiCz@{Jz@yBg@oU{OkCkCf@cLbBsIy@iCyGeB}H{@
mCnFoAvB}ReEyGaIpFsSx@iHoAmCkHkCQ{JmM{TS_DvBuG?qFR{@vBoA~Hg
@bBoAlCuL}@cG_IcGyEi@?sNUy@{@}@wLvBuB?aIcGgTgOSwLS_DoFoFwQTs
DUg^kW}Hwe@U_DrI_l@l@_Dx@g@fTbBjC?j\\sDlOgEdJcGnAwBaB{EuDoAaLc
B}J{JqDjCee@wGsD{JoAwB_X?cB{@g@g@kCqSkf@ye@gJkWoi@_]{JgESkHcB
kHco@u[{Od@{@e@sIa]{@gJk\\kMkHoF_NgJcG?oAaBoAyGcBoAgESgYvG{@?w
B_NcBgO~HoFrI_I~a@_]rNcVzJoAnU_q@nA{@rIsDrDsIwG_Ng@}CjMa]bBcGz
@g@nFl@z@i@sDa[vGiYvBoAfJ_Dz@_DgEoKoA_NdBuL`VkWvLmH_Ie@kH?wB
lCe^lTyBx@cL?f@{T{@yEcQyBoFfEoKtDeJPmCoFg@{@gO}Huj@oA}OgOaBeB
```

```
wQf@}@?mFsIyB_DyE_DaXrDcGrDbBkCvBgE{JsSoKsIqDSuDkHR{@xB?lAbBcB
R",

  levels:
"P?CFDEADGDHBGIBDCEADCFDECFADFBFGCFCEEBDBCDGBEBFHDEABDF
BCCDEBFCEFEDCFFECFGEFFCGEHEDCJFGDEDFGHDFBEGECFCIBEGCEDFF
GHEFCGEKFECGEHDEFGCEIFDEFGHGHIFDEFGDFGEFJDFEDGEFDGHFEGEF
IDEFBDGDFEFGHBDFDGLEFEGDHGDIDCFGHFGDEDFGDHEFGDBFJFHEFEIF
CGKGEHEDFDEGCIEFGHFGICFEGDHJCECFGDHDFEGIFEFDGDHFDGEFGICF
HFDGCJDEGEDEMFDGBDEP",

  zoomFactor: 2,

  numLevels: 18
});




map.addOverlay(pl);




  }

  }




function mapClick(marker, point) {

    if (!marker) {

        addRoutePoint(point);

    }

  }
```

```
function addRoutePoint(point) {

    var dist = 0;


    if (!routePoints[lineIx]) {

        routePoints[lineIx] = Array();

        routeMarkers[lineIx] = Array();

    }


    routePoints[lineIx].push(point);


    if (routePoints[lineIx].length > 1)   {

        plotRoute();

        dist = routePoints[lineIx][routePoints[lineIx].length-
2].distanceFrom(point) / 1000;

        totalDistance += dist;

        document.getElementById("dist").innerHTML = 'Total Distance: '+
totalDistance.toFixed(3) + ' km';

    }

    else {

        routeMarkers[lineIx][routePoints[lineIx].length-1] = new
GMarker(point,{icon:greenIcon,title:'Start'});

        map.addOverlay(routeMarkers[lineIx][routePoints[lineIx].length-1]);
```

```
        }
    document.getElementById("route").innerHTML += point.y.toFixed(6) + ' ' +
point.x.toFixed(6) + ' : ' + dist.toFixed(3) +"<br>";

}




function getMapcenter() {

        var center = map.getCenter();

        var z = map.getZoom();

        document.getElementById("coords").innerHTML = 'Map center:<br>' +
center.y.toFixed(6) + ' ' + center.x.toFixed(6) + '<br>Zoom: ' + z;

}




function DEC2DMS(dec) {


        var deg = Math.floor(Math.abs(dec));

        var min = Math.floor((Math.abs(dec)-deg)*60);

        var sec = (Math.round(((((Math.abs(dec) - deg) - (min/60)) * 60 * 60) * 100)
/ 100 ) ;


        deg = dec < 0 ? deg * -1 : deg;


        var dms  = deg + '&deg ' + min + '\' ' + sec + '"';
```

```
        return dms;

}


function plotRoute() {

    if (routeOverlays[lineIx]) {

        map.removeOverlay(routeOverlays[lineIx]);

    }

    routeOverlays[lineIx] = new GPolyline(routePoints[lineIx],'#C602C8',3,1);

    map.addOverlay(routeOverlays[lineIx]);


}

function clearAll() {

    while (lineIx > 0) {

        resetRoute();

    }


    totalDistance = 0;

    document.getElementById("dist").innerHTML = '';

    document.getElementById("route").innerHTML = 'Route points:<br>';

}



function resetRoute() {

    if (!routePoints[lineIx] || routePoints[lineIx].length == 0) {

        lineIx--;
```

```
        }


        routePoints[lineIx] = null;
        if (routeOverlays[lineIx]) {
                map.removeOverlay(routeOverlays[lineIx]);
        }


        for (var n = 0 ; n < routeMarkers[lineIx].length ; n++ ) {
                var marker = routeMarkers[lineIx][n];
                if (marker) {
                        map.removeOverlay(marker);
                }
        }
        routeMarkers[lineIx] = null;


        var html = document.getElementById("route").innerHTML;
        html = html.replace(/<br>[^<]+<br>$/,'<br>');
        document.getElementById("route").innerHTML = html;


}


function undoPoint() {
        if (!routePoints[lineIx] || routePoints[lineIx].length == 0) {
                lineIx--;
        }
```

```
        if (routePoints[lineIx].length > 1)   {


                var dist = routePoints[lineIx][routePoints[lineIx].length-
2].distanceFrom(routePoints[lineIx][routePoints[lineIx].length-1]) / 1000;

                totalDistance -= dist;

                document.getElementById("dist").innerHTML = 'Total Distance: '+
totalDistance.toFixed(3) + ' km';


                var html = document.getElementById("route").innerHTML;

                html = html.replace(/<br>[^<]+<br>(<br>)*$/,'<br>');

                document.getElementById("route").innerHTML = html;


                if (routeMarkers[lineIx][routePoints[lineIx].length-1]) {
                        var marker = routeMarkers[lineIx].pop();
                        if (marker) {
                                map.removeOverlay(marker);
                        }
                }
                routePoints[lineIx].pop();
                plotRoute();
        }
        else {
                resetRoute();
        }
}
```

```
function showPoints(xml) {

    var html = '';

    if (xml) {

        html = '<?xml version=\"1.0\" encoding=\"ISO-8859-1\"?>\n';


        html += '<routes>\n';

        for (var i = 0 ; i < lineIx ; i++ ) {

            html += ' <route>\n';

            for (var n = 0 ; n < routePoints[i].length ; n++ ) {

                html += '  <p lat="' + routePoints[i][n].y.toFixed(8) + '"
lon="' + routePoints[i][n].x.toFixed(8) + '"';

                if (routeMarkers[i][n]) {

                    html += ' markerIcon="'+
routeMarkers[i][n].getIcon().image +'"';

                }

                html += ' />\n';

            }


            html += ' </route>\n';

        }

        html += '</routes>\n';

    }

    else {

        for (var i = 0 ; i < lineIx ; i++ ) {

            for (var n = 0 ; n < routePoints[i].length ; n++ ) {

                html += routePoints[i][n].y.toFixed(8) + ', ' +
routePoints[i][n].x.toFixed(8) + '\n';
```

```
                }

        html += '----- new line ------ \n';

        }

}


if (html == '') {

    html += 'You must add a closing point to each line\n\n';

}


html += '\n\n';
//    html += encodePolyline();


var nWin =
window.open('','nWin','width=780,height=500,left=50,top=50,resizable=1,scrollbar
s=yes,menubar=no,status=no');

    nWin.focus();

    nWin.document.open ('text/xml\n\n');

    nWin.document.write(html);

    nWin.document.close();

}


function addIntermediate() {

    if (routePoints[lineIx].length > 1)   {

        if (routeMarkers[lineIx][routePoints[lineIx].length-1]) {


map.removeOverlay(routeMarkers[lineIx][routePoints[lineIx].length-1]);

        }
```

```
        routeMarkers[lineIx][routePoints[lineIx].length-1] = new
GMarker(routePoints[lineIx][routePoints[lineIx].length-
1],{icon:yellowIcon,title:'Point '+ routePoints[lineIx].length-1});

        map.addOverlay(routeMarkers[lineIx][routePoints[lineIx].length-1]);

    }

}




function addClosing() {

    if (routePoints[lineIx].length > 1)   {

        if (routeMarkers[lineIx][routePoints[lineIx].length-1]) {

    map.removeOverlay(routeMarkers[lineIx][routePoints[lineIx].length-1]);

        }

        routeMarkers[lineIx][routePoints[lineIx].length-1] = new
GMarker(routePoints[lineIx][routePoints[lineIx].length-
1],{icon:redIcon,title:'End'});

        map.addOverlay(routeMarkers[lineIx][routePoints[lineIx].length-1]);

        lineIx++;

        document.getElementById("route").innerHTML += '<br>';


    }



    var divs = document.getElementsByTagName('DIV');

    for (var n = 0 ; n < divs.length ; n++ ) {

        if (divs[n].className == 'gmnoprint') {

            divs[n].className = '';

        }
```

```
        }




}




//-----------------------------------------
function encodePolyline() {
    var encodedPoints = '';
    var    encodedLevels = '';

    var plat = 0;
    var plng = 0;

    for (var n = 0 ; n < routePoints[lineIx].length ; n++ ) {
        var lat = routePoints[lineIx][n].y.toFixed(8);
        var lng = routePoints[lineIx][n].x.toFixed(8);

        var level = (n == 0 || n == routePoints[lineIx].length-1) ? 3 : 1;
        var level = 0;

        var late5 = Math.floor(lat * 1e5);
```

```
        var lnge5 = Math.floor(lng * 1e5);


        dlat = late5 - plat;
        dlng = lnge5 - plng;


        plat = late5;
        plng = lnge5;


        encodedPoints += encodeSignedNumber(dlat) +
encodeSignedNumber(dlng);
        encodedLevels += encodeNumber(level);

    }



    var html = '';
    html += 'new GPolyline.fromEncoded({\n';
    html += ' color: "#0000ff",\n';
    html += ' weight: 4,\n';
    html += ' opacity: 0.8,\n';
    html += ' points: "'+encodedPoints+'",\n';
    html += ' levels: "'+encodedLevels+'",\n';
    html += ' zoomFactor: 16,\n';
    html += ' numLevels: 4\n';
    html += '});\n';


    return html;
```

```
}


function encodeSignedNumber(num) {
    var sgn_num = num << 1;

    if (num < 0) {
        sgn_num = ~(sgn_num);
    }


    return(encodeNumber(sgn_num));
}


// Encode an unsigned number in the encode format.
function encodeNumber(num) {
    var encodeString = "";

    while (num >= 0x20) {
        encodeString += (String.fromCharCode((0x20 | (num & 0x1f)) + 63));
        num >>= 5;
    }

    encodeString += (String.fromCharCode(num + 63));
    return encodeString;
}
```

//]]>

</script>

</head>

<body onload="load()" onunload="GUnload()">

    <div id="header" style="color: #FFFFC0; font: normal 14px verdana; padding:3px; margin:10px;">

    </div>

    <div id="msg" style="width: 680px; font: bold 12px verdana;padding:3px;margin:10px;">

<PRE><B>
GPS and Routes</br></P>

This pages shows the different routes that you may opt, to go to a specific place</br>

 <B>Instructions</B>

Click on any place, on the spot, and click several points, on the route, you may opt to destination</br>

On end of route, click, closing point

Click clear to restart again

Undo last: for removing the last point plotted

Show points txt will load a text file, showing the GPS points plotted

Show points xml, will load an xml file, showing the GPS points plotted

Click to upload: prompts uploading of GPS file, & returns your location from GPS
</PRE>

</div>


```
<FORM ACTION = "clsUpload.asp" ENCTYPE="multipart/form-data"
METHOD="POST">

File Name: <INPUT TYPE=FILE NAME="txtFile"><P>

<INPUT TYPE = "SUBMIT" NAME="cmdSubmit" VALUE="SUBMIT">

</FORM>


<INPUT type='button' name='Button1' value='Load point!'
onclick="window.location='http://aspspider.ws/universityproject/gpsloadmodule.as
p'">


<P>


<%

set o = new clsUpload

if o.Exists("cmdSubmit") then


'get client file name without path

sFileSplit = split(o.FileNameOf("txtFile"), "\")

sFile = sFileSplit(Ubound(sFileSplit))


o.FileInputName = "txtFile"

o.FileFullPath = Server.MapPath(".") & "\" & sFile

o.save
```

```
if o.Error = "" then

        response.write "Success. File saved to  " & o.FileFullPath & ". Demo Input =
" & o.ValueOf("Demo")


else

        response.write "Failed due to the following error: " & o.Error

end if


end if

set o = nothing

%>



<PRE>



<b><font color="black">Table of contents: </b> <b><a
href="mapstoggle.html"><font color="red">MAPS</a> </b> <b><a
href="routes.asp"><font color="red">GPS & ROUTES</a></b> <b><font
color="white"><a href="viewprocess.asp"><font
color="red">INFORMATION</a></b> <b><font color="white"><a
href="enterforum.asp"><font color="red">FORUM & FAQS </a></b> <b><font
color="white"><a href="login.html"><font color="red">DATABASE
ADMINISTRATION </a></b> <b><font color="white"><a
href="contact.html"><font color="red">CONTACT US </a></b> <b><font
```

```
color="white"><a href="uopproject.html"><font color="red">RETURN TO MAIN
PAGE </a></b> </PRE>

<font color="black"> </div>  <table cellspacing="0" cellpadding="0" style="-moz-
outline-width:8px; -moz-outline-radius:15px; -moz-outline-style:solid;-moz-
outline-color:#838FBB;margin:20px;">

        <tr>


            <td valign="top">

                <div id="map"></div>

            </td>
            <td valign="top">
                <div class="buttons">

                        <div class="buttonB" onclick="clearAll()">Clear
all</div>

                        <div class="buttonB" onclick="undoPoint()">Undo
last</div>

                        <div class="buttonB" onclick="addIntermediate()"
style="background: url('yellowSquare.png') no-repeat;background-position:5px
center;background-color:#F6D84C">Medium Pt.</div>



                        <div class="buttonB" onclick="addClosing()"
style="background: url('redCircle.png') no-repeat;background-position:5px
center;background-color:#F6D84C">Closing Pt.</div>

                        <div class="buttonB" onclick="showPoints()">Show
Points TXT</div>

                        <div class="buttonB"
onclick="showPoints(1)">Show Points XML</div>


                </div>
```

```html
                    <div class="wText" id="coords"></div>
                    <div class="wText" id="dist"></div>


                    <div class="wText" id="route">Route points:<br></div>
            </td>
        </tr>
    </table>
<br><br><br><br><br><br>
<script src="http://www.google-analytics.com/urchin.js" type="text/javascript">
</script>
<script type="text/javascript">
_uacct = "UA-1221628-1";
urchinTracker();
</script>


</body>
</html>
```

SAVEPROCESS

```
<%

Dim Conn

Dim Rs

Dim sql

'create connection

Set Conn = Server.CreateObject("ADODB.Connection")

Set Rs = Server.CreateObject("ADODB.Recordset")

Conn.Provider="Microsoft.Jet.OLEDB.4.0"

conn.Open
"c:\MemberSites\MemberSites_AspSpider_Ws\universityproject\database\gpsdatab
ase.mdb"

sql= "SELECT name, address, tel, lat, lng, type, region FROM records;"

'Set the lock and cursor type

Rs.CursorType = 2

Rs.LockType = 3

Rs.Open sql, Conn     'Open the recordset with sql query

Rs.AddNew 'Prepare the database to add a new record and add

Rs.Fields("name") = Request.Form("name")

Rs.Fields("address") = Request.Form("address")

Rs.Fields("tel") = Request.Form("tel")

Rs.Fields("lat") = Request.Form("lat")

Rs.Fields("lng") = Request.Form("lng")

Rs.Fields("type") = Request.Form("type")
```

```
Rs.Fields("region") = Request.Form("region")


Rs.Update   'Save the update

Rs.Close

Set Rs = Nothing

Set Conn = Nothing

%>
```

UOPPROJECT

```
<!DOCTYPE HTML PUBLIC "-//W3C//DTD HTML 4.01 Transitional//EN">

<html>

<!-- Created with the CoffeeCup HTML Editor 2008 -->

<!--        http://www.coffeecup.com/        -->

<!--        Brewed on 04/05/2009 20:33:50        -->

<head>

  <title>GPS and Back Pakers in Mauritius</title>

  <meta http-equiv="content-type" content="text/html;charset=utf-8" />

  <meta name="generator" content="CoffeeCup HTML Editor 2008 -
www.coffeecup.com">

  <meta name="description" content="">

  <meta name="keywords" content="">

</head>

<style type="text/css">

body

{

background:url(morne12.jpg) no-repeat;
```

}

</style>

<font color="white">Welcome to Mauritius, the paradise island.</font>

<font color="white">Mauritius is a fascinating country, often spoken as a paradise, and seen as a fairytale, with whitish beaches warm lagoon waters, all within the safe, richness of our coral reefs. We have excellent communication channels, cellular phone links to all parts of the island, high speed internet bandwidth, excellent lodging service, road networks, and a free democratic political stability. As a tropical island, we foster indigenous plants and exotic green environment and that dazzles Europeans and people living far from the tropics.

<font color="white">with the warmest cloth of welcome, we open our tropical island to visitors and foreigners, all across the globe, offering traditional services, as well as modern tourism facilities. To discover more, we invite you, through the website, a cliche of images of activities and the natural countryside.</font>

<P><font color="pink"><strong> Mauritius, at a glance </strong></font></P>

<font color="white">The island, is of volcanic origin,with mountains and hills and with fertile soils in the centre, covered with soothing green vegetation.</font>

<font color="white">The waters in our lagoons, are homes for a variety of corals, fish and marine life, much to the joy of divers and swimmers</font>

<font color="white">The temperature variation, is around 10 degrees in winter, to 35 in summer season</font>

<font color="white">Mauritius' main economy relies on sugar production, textile maufacturing, finance and the tourism industry. </font>

<font color="white">We have a blend of cultures, of asian people, as well as chinese and europeans, mixed into a splendour of cultures and traditions. </font>

<font color="white">Our democracy brings to us, an elected president, with an elected legislature. </font>

<P><b><font color="white">Table of contents </p></b>

<P><b><a href="mapstoggle.html"><font color="white">MAPS</a></p>

<P><b><a href="routes.asp"><font color="white">GPS & ROUTES</a></p>

<P><b><font color="white"><a href="viewprocess.asp"><font color="white">INFORMATION</a></p>

<P><b><font color="white"><a href="enterforum.asp"><font color="white">FORUM & FAQS </a></p>

<P><b><font color="white"><a href="login.html"><font color="white">DATABASE ADMINISTRATION </a></p>

<P><b><font color="white"><a href="contact.html"><font color="white">CONTACT US </a></p>

<pre>

</pre>
<pre><a href="http://pages.intnet.mu/yasir/myalbum.html"><font color="white">Gallery</a>   <a href="http://goafrica.about.com/library/bl.mapfacts.mauritius.htm"><font color="white">Facts of mauritius</a>   <a href="http://pages.intnet.mu/yasir/links.html"><font color="white">Links</a>   <a href="http://pages.intnet.mu/yasir/weather.html"><font color="white">weather</a>   <a href="http://www.airmauritius.com"><font color="white">Airliners</a></pre>

</body>

```
</html>
```

UPDATE

```
<html>

<body>

<%


'create connection

set conn=Server.CreateObject("ADODB.Connection")

conn.Provider="Microsoft.Jet.OLEDB.4.0"

conn.Open
"C:\MemberSites\MemberSites_AspSpider_Ws\universityproject\database\gpsdatab
ase.mdb"

set rs=Server.CreateObject("ADODB.Recordset")

rs.open "SELECT * FROM records",conn

%>


<h2>List of Database</h2>

<table border="1" width="100%">

<tr>

<PRE>




<b><font color="black">Table of contents: </b> <b><a
href="mapstoggle.html"><font color="red">MAPS</a> </b> <b><a
href="routes.asp"><font color="red">GPS & ROUTES</a></b> <b><font
color="white"><a href="viewprocess.asp"><font
color="red">INFORMATION</a></b> <b><font color="white"><a
```

```
href="enterforum.asp"><font color="red">FORUM & FAQS </a></b> <b><font
color="white"><a href="login.html"><font color="red">DATABASE
ADMINISTRATION </a></b> <b><font color="white"><a
href="contact.html"><font color="red">CONTACT US </a></b> <b><font
color="white"><a href="uopproject.html"><font color="red">RETURN TO MAIN
PAGE </a></b> </PRE>

<PRE>

<%

for each x in rs.Fields

  response.write("<th>" & ucase(x.name) & "</th>")

next

%>

</tr>

<% do until rs.EOF %>

<tr>

<form method="post" action="updateprocess.asp">

<%

for each x in rs.Fields

  if lcase(x.name)="name" then%>

    <td>

    <input type="submit" name="name" value="<%=x.value%>">

    </td>

  <%else%>

    <td><%Response.Write(x.value)%></td>

  <%end if

next

%>

</form>
```

```
<%rs.MoveNext%>

</tr>

<%

loop

conn.close

%>

</table>


</body>

</html>
```

UPDATE DATA

```html
<html>

<head>

<title> Enter data </title>

<script type="text/javascript">

<!--

function validate()

{

  if(document.form.type.address.length<4)

  {

  alert("Address too short");

  return false;

  }

  if(document.form.type.tel.length<9)

  {

  alert("invalid phone num");
```

```
  return false;
  }
 if(document.form.type.lat.length<7)
 {
  alert("Latitude lacks precision");
  return false;
 }
 if(document.form.type.lng.length<7)
 {
  alert("Longitude lacks precision");
  return false;
 }
 if(document.form.type.type.length<7)
 {
  alert("Too short type, enter either hotel, restaurant, or Fuel");
  return false;
 }
 else
 {
  return true;
 }
}
//-->
</script>
</head>
<body>
```

```
<form name="form" method="post" action="updatesave.asp">

<PRE>

<br>Address      : <input type="text" name="address" maxlength="50"> </br>

<br>Telephone    : <input type="text" name="tel" maxlength="9"> </br>

<br>Latitude     : <input type="text" name="lat" maxlength="10"> </br>

<br>Longitude    : <input type="text" name="lng" maxlength="10"> </br>

<br>Region       : <input type="text" name="region" maxlength="20"> </br>

<br>Type         : <input type="text" name="type" maxlength="10"> </br>

<br><input type="submit" name="Save" value="Submit" onClick="return
validate();"> </br>

</PRE>

<PRE>




<b><font color="black">Table of contents: </b> <b><a
href="mapstoggle.html"><font color="red">MAPS</a> </b> <b><a
href="routes.asp"><font color="red">GPS & ROUTES</a></b> <b><font
color="white"><a href="viewprocess.asp"><font
color="red">INFORMATION</a></b> <b><font color="white"><a
href="enterforum.asp"><font color="red">FORUM & FAQS </a></b> <b><font
color="white"><a href="login.html"><font color="red">DATABASE
ADMINISTRATION </a></b> <b><font color="white"><a
href="contact.html"><font color="red">CONTACT US </a></b> <b><font
color="white"><a href="uopproject.html"><font color="red">RETURN TO MAIN
PAGE </a></b> </PRE>

<PRE>


</form>

</body>
```

```
</html>
```

UPDATEPROCESS

```
<html>

<body>


<h2>Update Process</h2>

<%


'create connection

set conn=Server.CreateObject("ADODB.Connection")

conn.Provider="Microsoft.Jet.OLEDB.4.0"

conn.Open
"C:\MemberSites\MemberSites_AspSpider_Ws\universityproject\database\gpsdatab
ase.mdb"



cid=Request.Form("name")


if Request.form("name")="" then

  set rs=Server.CreateObject("ADODB.Recordset")

  rs.open "SELECT * FROM records WHERE name='" & cid & "'",conn

  %>

  <form method="post" action="updatedata.asp">
```

```
<table>
<%for each x in rs.Fields%>
<tr>
<td><%=x.name%></td>
<td><input name="<%=x.name%>" value="<%=x.value%>"></td>
<%next%>
</tr>
</table>
<br /><br />
<input type="submit" value="Update record">
</form>
<%
else
  sql="UPDATE records SET "
  sql=sql & "name='" & Request.Form("name") & "',"

  on error resume next
  conn.Execute sql
  if err<>0 then
    response.write("No update permissions!")
  else
    response.write("Record " & cid & " was updated!")
  end if
end if
conn.close
%>
```

```
</body>

</html>
```

UPDATESAVE

```
<%

Dim Conn

Dim Rs

Dim sql


'create connection

Set Conn = Server.CreateObject("ADODB.Connection")

Set Rs = Server.CreateObject("ADODB.Recordset")

Conn.Provider="Microsoft.Jet.OLEDB.4.0"

conn.Open
"c:\MemberSites\MemberSites_AspSpider_Ws\universityproject\database\gpsdatab
ase.mdb"

sql= "SELECT name region FROM records;"

'Set the lock and cursor type

Rs.CursorType = 2

Rs.LockType = 3

Rs.Open sql, Conn     'Open the recordset with sql query

Rs.AddNew 'Prepare the database to add a new record and add

Rs.Fields("name") = Request.Form("name")

Rs.Fields("address") = Request.Form("address")
```

```
Rs.Fields("tel") = Request.Form("tel")

Rs.Fields("lat") = Request.Form("lat")

Rs.Fields("lng") = Request.Form("lng")

Rs.Fields("type") = Request.Form("type")

Rs.Fields("region") = Request.Form("region")


Rs.Update   'Save the update

Rs.Close

Set Rs = Nothing

Set Conn = Nothing

%>
```

VIEWPROCESS

```
<%@LANGUAGE=VBScript%>

<%

' Define variables

dim recordsonpage, requestrecords, offset, allrecords, hiddenrecords, showrecords,
lastrecord, recordcounter, pagelist, pagelistcounter

' create connection

dim Conn

Set Conn = Server.CreateObject("ADODB.Connection")

Set Rs = Server.CreateObject("ADODB.Recordset")

Conn.Provider="Microsoft.Jet.OLEDB.4.0"

Conn.Open
"c:\MemberSites\MemberSites_AspSpider_Ws\universityproject\database\gpsdatab
ase.mdb"

' records per page

recordsonpage = 5
```

```
' count all records
allrecords = 0
set rs = Conn.Execute("SELECT * FROM records")
do until rs.EOF
  allrecords = allrecords + 1
  rs.movenext
loop
' if offset is zero then the first page will be loaded
offset = request.querystring("offset")
if offset = 0 OR offset = "" then
  requestrecords = 0
else
  requestrecords = requestrecords + offset
end if
' opens database
set rs = Conn.Execute("SELECT * FROM records ORDER BY name")
' reads first records (offset)
hiddenrecords = requestrecords
do until hiddenrecords = 0 OR rs.EOF
  hiddenrecords = hiddenrecords - 1
  rs.movenext
  if rs.EOF then
    lastrecord = 1
  end if
loop
```

```
%>
```

```html
<html>
 <head>
  <title>View process</title>
  <meta http-equiv="author" content="ny">
 </head>
<body>
```

```html
<table cellspacing="2" cellpadding="2" border="1" width="400">
```

```
<%
' prints records in the table
showrecords = recordsonpage
recordcounter = requestrecords
do until showrecords = 0 OR rs.EOF
recordcounter = recordcounter + 1
%>
```

```html
<tr>
 <td><b><% = recordcounter %></b></td>
 <td><% = rs("name") %></td>
 <td><% = rs("address") %></td>
</tr>
```

```
<%
```

```
showrecords = showrecords - 1

rs.movenext

if rs.EOF then

  lastrecord = 1

end if

loop

%>
```

```
</table>
```

```
<p>
```

```
<table cellspacing="2" cellpadding="2" border="1" width="400">

 <tr>

  <td><% if requestrecords <> 0 then %><a href="viewprocess.asp?offset=<% =
requestrecords - recordsonpage %>">Prev Page</a><% else %>Prev Page<% end if
%></td>

  <td><% if lastrecord <> 1 then %>   <a href="viewprocess.asp?offset=<% =
requestrecords + recordsonpage %>">Next Page</a><% else %>Next Page<% end
if %></td>

 </tr>

 <tr>

  <td colspan="2">pagelist:

<%

pagelist = 0

pagelistcounter = 0

do until pagelist > allrecords
```

```
  pagelistcounter = pagelistcounter + 1

%>

<a href="viewprocess.asp?offset=<% = pagelist %>"><% = pagelistcounter
%></a>

<%

  pagelist = pagelist + recordsonpage

loop

%>

  </td>

 </tr>

</table>

<PRE>




<b><font color="black">Table of contents: </b> <b><a
href="mapstoggle.html"><font color="red">MAPS</a> </b> <b><a
href="routes.asp"><font color="red">GPS & ROUTES</a></b> <b><font
color="white"><a href="viewprocess.asp"><font
color="red">INFORMATION</a></b> <b><font color="white"><a
href="enterforum.asp"><font color="red">FORUM & FAQS </a></b> <b><font
color="white"><a href="login.html"><font color="red">DATABASE
ADMINISTRATION </a></b> <b><font color="white"><a
href="contact.html"><font color="red">CONTACT US </a></b> <b><font
color="white"><a href="uopproject.html"><font color="red">RETURN TO MAIN
PAGE </a></b> </PRE>

<PRE>


<%

' Closes connection
```

rs.close

Conn.close

%>

</body>

</html>

VIEWPROCESSADMIN

<%@LANGUAGE=VBScript%>

<%

' Define variables

dim recordsonpage, requestrecords, offset, allrecords, hiddenrecords, showrecords, lastrecord, recordcounter, pagelist, pagelistcounter

' create connection

dim Conn

Set Conn = Server.CreateObject("ADODB.Connection")

Set Rs = Server.CreateObject("ADODB.Recordset")

Conn.Provider="Microsoft.Jet.OLEDB.4.0"

Conn.Open
"c:\MemberSites\MemberSites_AspSpider_Ws\universityproject\database\gpsdatab
ase.mdb"

' records per page

recordsonpage = 5

' count all records

allrecords = 0

set rs = Conn.Execute("SELECT * FROM records")

do until rs.EOF

```
    allrecords = allrecords + 1

    rs.movenext

loop


' if offset is zero then the first page will be loaded

offset = request.querystring("offset")

if offset = 0 OR offset = "" then

  requestrecords = 0

else

  requestrecords = requestrecords + offset

end if


' opens database

set rs = Conn.Execute("SELECT * FROM records ORDER BY name")


' reads first records (offset)

hiddenrecords = requestrecords

do until hiddenrecords = 0 OR rs.EOF

  hiddenrecords = hiddenrecords - 1

  rs.movenext

  if rs.EOF then

    lastrecord = 1

  end if

loop

%>
```

```
<html>
 <head>
  <title>View process</title>
  <meta http-equiv="author" content="ny">
 </head>
<body>

<table cellspacing="2" cellpadding="2" border="1" width="400">

<%
' prints records in the table
showrecords = recordsonpage
recordcounter = requestrecords
do until showrecords = 0 OR rs.EOF
recordcounter = recordcounter + 1
%>

 <tr>
  <td><b><% = recordcounter %></b></td>
  <td><% = rs("name") %></td>
  <td><% = rs("address") %></td>
 </tr>

<%
 showrecords = showrecords - 1
 rs.movenext
```

```
 if rs.EOF then

  lastrecord = 1

 end if

loop

%>


</table>


<p>


<table cellspacing="2" cellpadding="2" border="1" width="400">

 <tr>

  <td><% if requestrecords <> 0 then %><a
href="viewprocessadmin.asp?offset=<% = requestrecords - recordsonpage
%>">Prev Page</a><% else %>Prev Page<% end if %></td>

  <td><% if lastrecord <> 1 then %>   <a href="viewprocessadmin.asp?offset=<%
= requestrecords + recordsonpage %>">Next Page</a><% else %>Next Page<%
end if %></td>

 </tr>

 <tr>

  <td colspan="2">pagelist:

<%

pagelist = 0

pagelistcounter = 0

do until pagelist > allrecords

 pagelistcounter = pagelistcounter + 1

%>
```

```
<a href="viewprocessadmin.asp?offset=<% = pagelist %>"><% = pagelistcounter
%></a>

<%

  pagelist = pagelist + recordsonpage

loop

%>

  </td>

 </tr>

</table>


<%

' Closes connection

rs.close

Conn.close

%>


<INPUT type='button' name='Button1' value='Export to XML!'
onclick="window.location='http://aspspider.ws/universityproject/accesstoxml.asp'"
>


<INPUT type='button' name='Button1' value='View updated map!'
onclick="window.location='http://aspspider.ws/universityproject/mapstoggle.html'
">

<PRE>


<b><font color="black">Table of contents: </b> <b><a
href="mapstoggle.html"><font color="red">MAPS</a> </b> <b><a
href="routes.asp"><font color="red">GPS & ROUTES</a></b> <b><font
color="white"><a href="viewprocess.asp"><font
```

```
color="red">INFORMATION</a></b> <b><font color="white"><a
href="enterforum.asp"><font color="red">FORUM & FAQS </a></b> <b><font
color="white"><a href="login.html"><font color="red">DATABASE
ADMINISTRATION </a></b> <b><font color="white"><a
href="contact.html"><font color="red">CONTACT US </a></b> <b><font
color="white"><a href="uopproject.html"><font color="red">RETURN TO MAIN
PAGE </a></b> </PRE>
```

```
<PRE>
```

```
</body>
```

```
</html>
```

WEATHER

```
<head> Weather page, links of what available weather conditions are in mauritius
```

```
</head>
```

```
<body>
```

```
<b><p>Weather in Port Louis, the city of mauritius</b></p>
```

```
<iframe
src="http://news.bbc.co.uk/weather/forecast/993/Next3DaysEmbed.xhtml?target=_
parent" allowTransparency="true" width="306" height="435"
frameborder="0">You must have a browser that supports iframes to view the BBC
weather forecast</iframe>
```

```
<a
href="http://www.wunderground.com/global/stations/61990.html?bannertypeclick=
bigwx"><img
src="http://weathersticker.wunderground.com/weathersticker/bigwx_cond/language
```

/www/global/stations/61990.gif" alt="Click for Plaisance, Mauritius Forecast" border="0" height="60" width="468" /></a>

</head>

</body>

www.ingramcontent.com/pod-product-compliance
Lightning Source LLC
LaVergne TN
LVHW042333060326
832902LV00006B/144